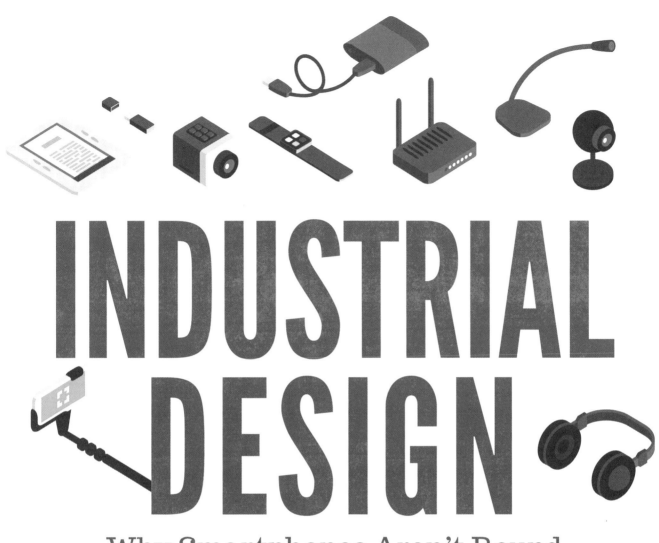

INDUSTRIAL DESIGN

Why Smartphones Aren't Round and Other Mysteries
with Science Activities for Kids

CARLA MOONEY
Illustrated by Tom Casteel

Titles in the **Technology Today** book set

  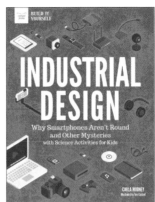 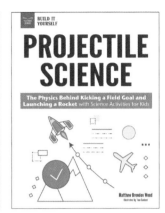

Check out more titles at www.nomadpress.net

Nomad Press
A division of Nomad Communications
10 9 8 7 6 5 4 3 2 1

This book was manufactured by Friesens Book Division
Altona, MB, Canada
August 2018, Job #244129

ISBN Softcover: 978-1-61930-672-1
ISBN Hardcover: 978-1-61930-670-7

Educational Consultant, Marla Conn

Questions regarding the ordering of this book should be addressed to
Nomad Press
2456 Christian St.
White River Junction, VT 05001
www.nomadpress.net

Printed in Canada.

Contents

Interested in Primary Sources?

 Look for this icon. Use a smartphone or tablet app to scan the QR code and explore more! Photos are also primary sources because a photograph takes a picture at the moment something happens.

If the QR code doesn't work, there's a list of URLs on the Resources page. Or, try searching the internet with the Keyword Prompts to find other helpful sources.

industrial design

1440: German Johannes Gutenberg creates the first printing press, which designers use to publish pattern books.

1700s–1900s: The Industrial Revolution introduces new ideas, factories, and manufacturing methods to cities around the world.

1851: Isaac Merit Singer designs and builds an improved sewing machine.

1859: Michael Thonet's classic café chair, the Model No. 14, becomes the first chair specifically designed for high-volume mass production.

1863: American James Plimpton designs a rocking roller skate that can turn.

1907: German company AEG recruits a German architect named Peter Behrens to improve the company's products and design.

1909: General Electric (GE) introduces its electric toaster.

1916: Coca Cola creates the iconic glass bottle for its soda, inspired by the gourd-shaped cocoa pod.

1919: Charles Strite patents his pop-up toaster, which he calls the Toastmaster.

1939: Swingline introduces an innovative stapler that allows users to open the top and easily drop in new staples.

1939–1945: World War II erupts and leads to government funding on research and development for cutting-edge manufacturing plants and state-of-the-art materials, which are later used for commercial products.

1945: American Earl Tupper introduces his line of plastic food storage containers called Tupperware.

1956: Ampex releases the world's first magnetic tape video recorder, the VRX-1000.

1963: American Ivan Sutherland develops Sketchpad, an innovative computer-aided design (CAD) software, while working at the Massachusetts Institute of Technology.

1974: American Art Fry overhears Dr. Spencer Silver talking about his invention—an adhesive that could be applied, removed, and applied again without damaging an object. Fry applies the adhesive to paper and creates the Post-it Note.

1977: The Atari 2600 is launched, creating excitement for the video game market.

1981: International Business Machines introduces the first personal computer, which marks the beginning of wide adoption of CAD software for design.

1985: Nintendo releases the Nintendo Entertainment System in the United States. It becomes the leading gaming console in the country for several years.

1998: Apple launches the iMac G3, a brightly colored, translucent computer.

2001: Apple introduces its new music player, the iPod.

2007: Apple launches the iPhone.

2014: The launch of the Apple Watch ushers in a new age of smartwatches and wearable devices.

2018: Virtual reality becomes an educational device for schoolchildren to learn about far-off places and things without having to leave the classroom!

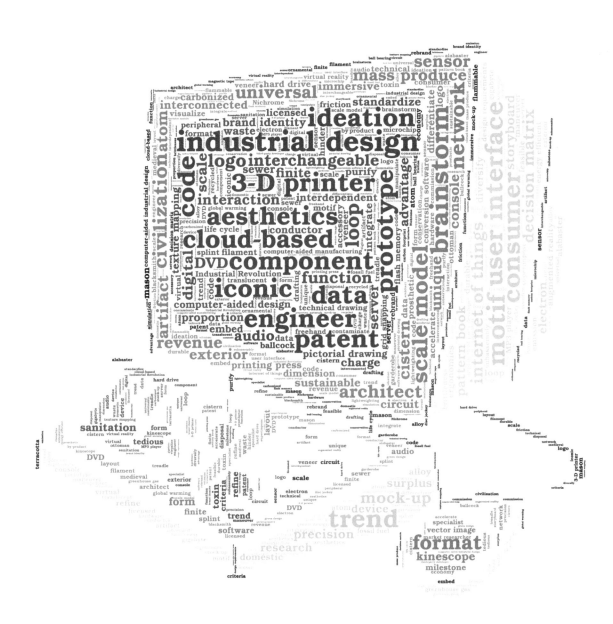

WHAT IS
INDUSTRIAL
DESIGN?

Do you have an MP3 player? Do you like using it? How could it be easier to use? How could the design of your MP3 player be improved?

Industrial design tackles questions such as these about lots of different products. **Engineers** and **designers** work to make things efficient, user-friendly, safe, and even beautiful. Why is this important? What would the world be like if we settled for objects that weren't easy to use? Is it necessary that the objects we use every day have beauty? Why or why not?

Let's take a look at what industrial design really is and what it takes to be an industrial designer. You might be surprised!

ESSENTIAL QUESTION

What objects have you used today that were influenced by industrial design?

WORDS TO KNOW

MP3 player: an electronic device that can play digital audio files.

industrial design: the process of designing goods for mass production.

engineer: a person who uses science, math, and creativity to design and build things.

designer: someone who plans the form, look, and workings of a product based on the experiences of the user.

civilization: a community of people that is advanced in art, science, and government.

Industrial Revolution: a period of time in the eighteenth and nineteenth centuries when large-scale production of goods began.

mass produce: to manufacture and assemble hundreds or thousands of the same product.

format: the way data is organized.

WHAT IS INDUSTRIAL DESIGN?

Since the earliest times, people have searched for better solutions to specific problems. They have tried to improve stone tools, cooking pots, weapons, and more. When creating each new item, they have thought hard about it—what problem are they trying to solve, what are they trying to accomplish, how can they make it work better? Answering these questions, they created a design. Through design, people have created the key inventions of our **civilization**.

Before the **Industrial Revolution**, which began during the 1700s, most goods were made by hand and designed by their crafters.

The assembly plant of the Bell Aircraft Corp. at Wheatfield, New York, c. 1940

Since the introduction of factories during the Industrial Revolution, many products are **mass produced**, such as airplanes, cars, and toasters. Individual parts are standardized and later assembled either by hand or other machines. This changed the role of design, separating the designers from producers.

The term "industrial designer" comes from designing products manufactured by industry.

Industrial design is the process of brainstorming and planning every aspect of a product before it is made in mass production. It includes making decisions about how a product is used by a person, what technologies it uses, the materials it is made from, and how it looks and feels. Industrial design is a problem-solving process. In the same way that the Apple team designed the iPod, industrial designers around the world solve problems and make products better.

An industrial designer is concerned about the interaction between an object and the user. Examples of industrial design are all around you, supporting and shaping your everyday life. The mobile phone in your pocket, the clock on your wall, the coffeemaker in your kitchen, and the chair you are sitting on are all products of industrial design. Everything manmade that you can see and touch was designed by someone, and thus influenced by industrial design.

Let's take a look at the invention of the iPod and learn how industrial design made it possible!

DID YOU KNOW?

There are more than 40,000 industrial designers working in the United States.

WHAT'S ON YOUR PLAYLIST?

In the 1990s, MP3 players were some of the newest gadgets on the market. An MP3 player is a small, handheld device that allows users to store and play music files in an MP3 **format**. Lots of people wanted to have one of these gadgets so they could listen to music on the go.

WORDS TO KNOW

device: a piece of equipment, such as a phone or MP3 player, that is made for a specific purpose.

flash memory: a type of memory chip that is used to store and transfer data between a computer and digital devices.

hard drive: a storage device for data.

hardware: the physical parts of an electronic device, such as the case, keyboard, screen, and speakers.

research: the planned investigation and study of something to discover facts and reach conclusions.

brainstorm: to think creatively and without judgment, often in a group of people.

data: information, often given in the form of numbers, that can be processed by a computer.

gigabyte (GB): a unit of information equal to 1 billion.

digital: data expressed in a series of the digits 0 and 1.

disc jockey: someone who plays recorded music at an event or on the radio.

Even though they were an exciting new product, MP3 players were not perfect. At the time, many of these **devices** used **flash memory**, which significantly limited the number of songs they could hold, often to no more than 12 or so. Some players had a **hard drive**, which held more songs, but this made the player a lot bigger and heavier. These larger hard drive players were also harder to use.

> **Even transferring music files to the MP3 player was not easy. It took about five minutes to transfer a dozen songs from a computer to an MP3 player.**

Moving thousands of songs could take several hours! Steve Jobs (1955–2011), the co-founder of Apple, believed the existing MP3 players left much to be desired. He decided that Apple should create a better MP3 player.

How we used to carry our music around!

BUILDING A TEAM

Jobs may have come up with the idea of designing a new MP3 player, but no single person created it for Apple. Instead, a team of Apple employees and other workers brought the idea to life. To start, Jobs assigned Jon Rubinstein (1956–), Apple's senior vice president of **hardware**, to the project.

Rubinstein began **researching** and **brainstorming** ideas for the new MP3 player. To improve the slow transfer speed of music files, he wanted to use an Apple technology called FireWire, which enabled **data** to be transferred at much faster speeds than with other technologies at the time. He also wanted to use a specific 1.8-inch, 5-**gigabyte (GB)** hard drive from computer-maker Toshiba. Its small size would make Apple's device smaller and lighter than other hard drive MP3 players.

Rubinstein brought in several people to help him develop the new player. He called Tony Fadell (1969–), who had lots of experience working with handheld computing devices and **digital** audio players. As a bonus, Fadell was also a devoted music fan who worked as a **disc jockey** in his free time. For every gig, Fadell dragged his massive collection of compact discs (CDs) along with him. Fadell was fascinated by the idea of creating a device that would make his job easier.

Rubinstein asked Fadell to come up with some designs for a new MP3 player. Fadell was to focus on how it could be built, what **components** it would use, and how much it would cost. For six weeks, Fadell met with many people in the handheld computing industry. He studied competitors' products. The entire time, he kept his project a secret.

Fadell worked to design a small, ultra-portable device with the ability to hold a lot of music files. Oh, and it had to have a long battery life, too.

CREATING A DESIGN

By the end of the six weeks, Fadell developed three **prototype** designs for Apple. The models were very rough, built using foam-core boards and fishing weights! Designers are constantly making various iterations of their ideas. Some may be simple paper models and others may be very realistic models that look and feel just like a finished product. In April 2001, Fadell presented his prototypes to Apple executives, including Steve Jobs.

At the same meeting, Phil Schiller (1960–), Apple's senior vice president of worldwide product marketing, presented **mock-ups** of a player that used a scroll wheel. Schiller believed the scroll wheel would make it easier for users to **manipulate** the player. In other MP3 players, users pressed plus and minus buttons to move, one song at a time, through their entire collection of music files. If a user had thousands of songs, they had to push the button thousands of times to find the one they wanted.

The first generation of iPod
credit: Jennie Robinson Faber (CC BY 2.0)

The scroll wheel, however, allowed users to spin through the list much more quickly with only a quick flick of the finger. And because Apple could make the scroll speed **accelerate** the longer a user spun the wheel, users could much more easily navigate through their songs at any rate they wanted. This is one of the main concerns of the industrial designer. How can a user interact with a device so that they can complete a task easily and naturally.

Jobs liked both Fadell's and Schiller's ideas and gave the green light to move forward. The top-secret project was called "P-68."

After consulting with Apple's marketing department, Fadell decided the new MP3 player needed to be ready for Christmas 2001. He had only six months to develop, manufacture, and ship the player. Fadell quickly gathered a team. Part of the team worked on the player's **software**, while another group worked on hardware.

iTunes Changes Music

In January 2001, Apple introduced iTunes, a music app that would change the way the world buys and listens to music. Before this, listening to a custom playlist of music was a multi-step process. People bought albums on CD, loaded the music onto computers, created playlists from different CDs, and then burned those playlists to new CDs. To listen to digital music on MP3 players before iTunes and iPods, users had to deal with complicated apps. Apple's iTunes, however, solved these problems. It allowed users to transform CDs into MP3 digital files and organize their music files with an easy **user interface**. Less than a year later, Apple introduced the iPod and released a new version of iTunes that seamlessly **integrated** with the iPod. In April 2003, iTunes 4 introduced the iTunes Music Store, where people could purchase digital music directly from Apple for 99 cents a song. The iTunes Music Store sold 1 million songs in its first week.

Team members put in long hours, working as much as 18 to 20 hours a day, seven days a week. They used a shoe-box-sized prototype, which made it easier to work on the invention and kept the ultimate size of the device a secret.

While the software and hardware teams worked, Apple's industrial design group, led by Jonathan Ive (1967–), designed the player's **exterior** appearance.

After testing dozens of prototypes, Ive's team chose a design. Weighing only 6 ounces, the new player looked like a simple box and held a tiny hard drive with 5 GB of storage, which could hold about 1,000 songs.

Apple's Sir Jonathan Ive

Technology company Apple is known for its innovative designs, including the iMac, iPod, iPhone, iPad, Apple Watch, and more. Jonathan Ive is Apple's chief design officer. Since 1996, Ive has led Apple's design team, one of the world's best. He and his team are responsible for all design at Apple, including the look and feel of Apple hardware, user interfaces, packaging, retail stores, and future projects.

Believing the computer has become the center of home life, Ive designs machines that are sleek, touchable, and appealing to display. He emphasizes ease and simplicity of use and devotes his attention to often overlooked details. For example, Ive's design for the 1996 iMac stunned consumers with its translucent candy colors, rounded exterior, and functional core. He shrank the computer's processor to fit inside its colorful shell, dramatically shrinking the computer's footprint. The sale of 2 million iMacs in 1998 gave Apple its first profitable year since 1995. Ive holds more than 5,000 **patents** and has received many design awards, including the Design Museum London's first Designer of the Year award in 2003. In 2013, Ive, a British citizen, was knighted for his design accomplishments and services to become Sir Jonathan Ive.

Ive chose a white plastic front that was set into a stainless steel case. He wanted the neutral white face and stainless steel case to set it apart from the current market of black and dark gray portable digital gadgets. The player's face featured a simple rectangular display, five buttons, and a scroll wheel. The scroll wheel was used to move through songs and adjust volume. It had no removable battery door, no on/off switch, and no screws. The player's sealed inner workings sent a simple, confident message to users—this device works.

At the time, selling **consumer** music gadgets was new for Apple. This was a company that sold computers. Apple's MP3 product would be for someone other than the traditional Apple customer. To help with sales, Apple brought in experts to design the player's marketing campaign. One of those experts, freelance copywriter Vinnie Chieco, came up with the player's name—the iPod.

DID YOU KNOW?

Industrial design can be influenced by the environment and the materials available.

Chieco imagined a spaceship as the ultimate hub from which a smaller craft—such as a pod—could come and go. While competitors marketed their products based on tech specs, Apple designed a marketing campaign that emphasized the iPod's style and fashion. It was a winning strategy.

After months of hard work, the iPod became a reality. Apple shipped the first iPods in November 2001. In a press release, Steve Jobs said that the iPod let users put their entire music collection in their pocket so they could listen to it wherever they went. Since then, Apple has sold more than 400 million iPods. While the iPod was not the world's first portable music player, its revolutionary design transformed the music industry and even changed how users listen to music.

Apple's iPod made music accessible to everyone. It will be remembered as one of the most significant successes of industrial design in history.

form: how something looks.

function: how something works. To work or operate in a particular, correct way.

ergonomics: the study of people and their working conditions.

aesthetics: a set of principles concerned with nature and the appreciation of beauty.

green design: an approach to design that minimizes harmful effects on human health and the environment.

WHY DESIGN MATTERS

Do you like how your MP3 player works? Would you buy from the same company again? The design of a product greatly affects its chances of success. Design is much more than creating a product that works. It's also creating a product that people want to use. If the design of your MP3 player isn't quite right and you feel uncomfortable or frustrated every time you use it, you probably won't buy that model again. You'll probably tell your friends not to buy it!

Industrial designers balance **form** with **function** every time they design a product. Good design combines the right materials, colors, details, and form to make you want to buy and use a product. They balance the needs and wants of the user with what is technologically possible and socially acceptable.

A good industrial designer puts the user's experience first.

When designing a product, they choose details that ensure users have the best experience possible. A well-designed product is easy to use and does what it is meant to do.

In this book, you'll study the design process behind the products we use every day, from blenders to lamps to laptops. You'll explore the design process from its earliest beginnings, when individuals designed and crafted their own tools, to today, when industrial designers work to find the best design for products that are then manufactured in bulk by machines. You'll practice engineering design skills and learn how to create useful, pleasing designs for a variety of products. Like a good designer, you will practice evaluating products for function, usability, **ergonomics**, **aesthetics**, and **green design**. Open up your notebook and let's get started with industrial design!

Industrial Design Process

Every designer keeps a notebook to keep track of their ideas and their steps in the industrial design process. As you read through this book and do the activities, keep track of your observations, data, and designs in a design worksheet, like the one shown here. When doing an activity, remember that there is no right answer or right way to approach a project. Be creative and have fun!

Problem: What problem are we trying to solve?
Research: Has anything been invented to help solve the problem? What can we learn?
Question: Are there any special requirements for the device? An example of this is a car that must go a certain distance in a certain amount of time.
Brainstorm: Draw lots of designs for your device and list the materials you are using!
Prototype: Build the design you drew during brainstorming.
Test: Test your prototype and record your observations.
Evaluate: Analyze your test results. Do you need to make adjustments? Do you need to try a different prototype?

Each chapter of this book begins with an essential question to help guide your exploration of industrial design. Keep the question in your mind as you read the chapter. At the end of each chapter, use your notebook to record your thoughts and answers.

ESSENTIAL QUESTION

What objects have you used today that were influenced by industrial design?

Keep a Design Notebook

Industrial designers often carry notebooks to capture their thoughts and ideas, no matter where they are. The best way to come up with a successful design is to have a lot of ideas first! Once a designer picks an idea to develop, he or she can use the design notebook to keep all of their thoughts and work in one place. They can record every detail about the project from start to finish in the notebook. They can record research, observations, ideas, sketches, and questions during the design process.

Many designers choose notebooks with blank or gridded pages because they can easily use them for sketches. Some designers prefer larger notebooks that can hold a lot of information, while others prefer smaller ones that are easier to carry. The choice is up to you!

❯ **In your design notebook, you can:**

* Make notes about problems you observe

* Brainstorm possible solutions to problems

* Make notes about background research

* Sketch different ideas and solutions

* Record interviews with users and/or experts

* Include photos of competitors' products

* Record a list of design requirements

* Write down questions or issues as they arise

To Explore More

Think about what other types of information you can keep in your design notebook? Why is this information important?

Chapter 1

FROM CRAFTSMANSHIP TO
MASS PRODUCTION

Even before factories and mass production, design was always an important part of making objects. There's nothing like using a well-designed, functional product exactly as it's meant to be used. This can spark a feeling of purpose and even joy. All from a well-designed product? Sure!

But the opposite is true, too. Using a product that isn't designed well and doesn't work correctly can be frustrating and even dangerous.

How do we ensure that there are more well-designed products out there than products that make us anxious when we have to use them? It's been a long, historical process of large and small steps toward a partnership between design and manufacturing.

ESSENTIAL QUESTION

Why did the world move from craft-based design to mass manufacturing?

WORDS TO KNOW

blacksmith: a person who makes things out of iron.

mason: a person who builds with stone or brick.

unique: special or unusual.

printing press: a machine that presses inked type onto paper.

artifact: an object made by people in the past, including tools, pottery, and jewelry.

CRAFT-BASED DESIGN

For many centuries, when people needed something, they either made it themselves or found someone to make it for them. Most products were made at home, by the people who used them. A few individuals specialized in making certain products, such as the village shoemaker who made shoes or the carpenter who built tables and chairs. Some towns relied on the skills of local craftsmen— **blacksmiths**, carpenters, **masons**, potters, and weavers, for example—for products they used every day.

DID YOU KNOW?

Leonardo's study of the natural world influenced his inventions and design. For example, Leonardo's carefully drawn studies of birds and bats influenced his designs of flying machines.

In early times, most products were handmade and **unique**, designed by those who made them. The craftsmen determined the form of the product as they created it. For example, a carpenter selected the type of wood to use for a table and the table's height and width as he carved and cut the wood.

One of the world's most famous artists, Leonardo da Vinci (1452–1519), was also admired for his inventive designs. He filled notebooks with thousands of drawings and diagrams related to concepts of math, science, and engineering.

Leonardo often used creativity and design to solve a problem. For example, back then, the cannons used by soldiers took a long time to load. To solve the problem, Leonardo designed a multi-barreled gun—a 33-barreled organ that could be loaded and fired simultaneously. He designed the 33-barreled organ from 33 connected small-caliber guns. The guns were separated into three rows of 11 guns each, all connected to a revolving platform with wheels.

All the guns could be loaded at the same time. During battle, soldiers could fire a single row of 11 guns. Then, they could rotate the wheeled platform to aim and fire the next row of guns. While they fired one row, another would be cooling, and the third could be loaded. This design allowed soldiers to fire repeatedly without stopping to reload.

Using his imagination and knowledge of how cannons worked, Leonardo was able to devise a new weapon for Italy to use against its enemies that was easy to use.

GUTENBERG'S PRINTING PRESS

One key step on the road to mass production was the **printing press**, first invented in 1440 by Johannes Gutenberg (c. 1398–1468). Developed in Strasbourg, Germany, the printing press led to the mass production of books.

Previously, books were handwritten and painstakingly copied, a long and tedious process that prevented books from reaching the masses. Instead, books were more like works of art or religious **artifacts** that were kept locked from the public.

After Gutenberg invented the printing press, thoughts, ideas, and words could be easily reproduced for the first time in history. Copies of books spread widely to many people.

A woodcut by Swiss artist Jost Amman (1539–1591) shows an early version of the printing press.

WORDS TO KNOW

milestone: an action or event marking a significant change or stage in development.

pattern book: a book containing samples of patterns and designs for furniture, cloth, and other objects.

motif: a decorative design or pattern.

ornamental: decorative.

economy: the way goods and services are bought and sold in a society.

In the world of industrial design, Gutenberg's press was a **milestone** invention. Before this, the process of design was tightly linked to the making of an object. With the printing press, designers could publish **pattern books** filled with furniture designs, metalwork designs, embroidery patterns, and other decorative **motifs**. Books for craftsmen had descriptions of techniques and instructions for making many different objects.

With these pattern books, the original designer did not need to be part of the making of a product. A craftsman who had the book could simply copy the design from its pages. The designing of a product was separating from the manufacturing of a product.

Design Patent

Designers spend a lot of time and money developing new products. They want to protect their ideas so other people and companies cannot use their designs without permission. What protects designers from having their work stolen? In the United States, a patent grants a designer a property right, which prevents other people from making and selling the same product for a number of years. A patent protects the way a product works, while a design patent protects the way it looks.

In 1842, U.S. patent laws were changed to allow for the patenting of **ornamental** designs. The design patent statute was amended in 1902 to cover any new and original ornamental design for a manufactured article. Ornamental designs of jewelry, furniture, beverage containers, and computer icons are examples of items covered by design patents. When a design patent is granted, an object with a design that is very similar to the design in the patent cannot be made, used, copied, or imported into the United States. In 1842, George Bruce (1781–1861) was awarded the first U.S. design patent for his creation of a new typeface.

INDUSTRIAL REVOLUTION

From the late 1700s through the early 1900s, things began to change. Many new ideas, inventions, and innovations dramatically affected the way people lived and worked. This era of great change was called the Industrial Revolution.

Factories full of machines sprang up in towns and cities. Steam engines and railroads carried goods to people who lived far away. Rapid improvements in manufacturing led to more goods being mass-produced in factories instead of being individually handcrafted.

DID YOU KNOW? All around Europe, workshops used models, pattern books, and published drawings to bring designs to life.

Growing economies, better transportation systems, and new large cities brought increased demands for factory-made goods.

Handcrafted goods could not keep up with the increased demand. Instead, craftsmen were called upon to design products that could be made by machines in large quantities. These craftsmen became some of the first industrial designers.

By 1800, England was home to factories that were mass-producing items such as pottery, spoons, buttons, buckles, and teapots. The Industrial Revolution began in Britain, and it soon spread to the rest of Europe and the United States.

In factories, the labor of making goods could be divided and performed by different groups of workers, instead of one craftsman working on an object from start to finish. Skilled laborers could be used in production instead of trained craftsmen. In this way, design became further separated from the act of making objects.

WORDS TO KNOW

advantage: something helpful.

specialist: a person who concentrates on a specific field or activity.

architect: a person who designs buildings.

domestic: related to the running of a home or family.

By the end of the nineteenth century, manufacturers began to realize that by improving the appearance and form of a product, they could gain an **advantage** against competitors. If people liked the way a product looked, and if it worked as expected, they were more likely to buy it.

As a result, manufacturers began to invite design **specialists**—often **architects**—to give advice and contribute to the design process. By the early twentieth century, many manufacturers recognized the importance of industrial design.

In 1859, Michael Thonet's (1796–1871) classic café chair became the first chair specifically designed for high-volume mass production. The Model No. 14 chair had a double-looped back and was simplified and stripped of ornamentation. Every part of its frame and seat was essential to its function. Thonet included only the key components of a chair. His simplified design significantly reduced both the material and labor costs of making the chair.

The design was perfectly matched to high-volume mass production.

Michael Thonet's original design looked very similar to these later versions.

The unassembled chairs were also easy to pack in boxes for shipment. People could assemble the chairs with a screwdriver! Because of their simple design, the chairs could be used in homes, hotels, restaurants, cafes, and bars. This was in essence the first IKEA chair. Thonet had designed the parts and transferred the assembly of the product to the consumer.

By 1891, an impressive 7.3 million chairs had been sold. The Model No. 14 showed that designing affordable products for mass production could be very profitable for manufacturers.

DID YOU KNOW?

Thonet's design was for a lightweight yet strong chair that cost less than a bottle of wine.

PETER BEHRENS: INDUSTRIAL DESIGNER

In the early 1900s, more manufacturers experimented with separating design from the manufacturing process. Around this time, a German company called AEG manufactured electric **domestic** appliances. In 1907, AEG recruited a German architect named Peter Behrens (1868–1940) to improve the company's products and design.

Behrens was responsible for every aesthetic decision at AEG. Behrens worked on AEG's products, including lamps, clocks, fans, and electric tea kettles. He sketched outlines and created product designs. He **standardized subassemblies** on many products, making the parts **interchangeable** among products. Because the parts could be used in several products instead of just one, production was more efficient and less costly.

Behrens gave AEG a new **brand identity** that helped its products stand out in the marketplace. Many of Behrens's designs for AEG were simple, yet they had a sophisticated artistic quality. For his work at AEG, Behrens is considered by many to be one of the world's first industrial designers.

One of the main ways AEG **differentiated** its products from the competition was by advertising them as original models of artistic design and examples of good taste. Behrens spread these messages through attractive posters and packaging and through storefronts with the same clean and simple design as the products he was advertising. He redesigned all of AEG's advertisements, exhibit brochures, and catalogs. He even designed a new **logo** for the company that appeared on factory buildings in various German cities.

DESIGN AND WAR

In the twentieth century, war had a significant impact on industrial design. In World War I, mass production of weapons changed warfare permanently, as designers focused on creating and improving tools for the war effort.

DID YOU KNOW?

One wartime design is the ballpoint pen. Pilots liked them more than fountain pens because they could use them at high altitudes!

Singer's Sewing Machine

While working in a Boston machine shop in 1851, Isaac Merit Singer (1811–1875) repaired a sewing machine and saw a way to improve its design. Within 11 days, Singer built a sewing machine that could be operated by a **treadle**. This is a lever pressed by the foot that drove the sewing machine's needle, allowing the user to have both hands free. Another attachment kept the material being sewed in place. Though both of these features had been used previously, Singer was the first to successfully use them in a practical sewing machine. Singer patented his design and formed the I.M. Singer & Co., which would later become the Singer Manufacturing Co., and began to manufacture the machine. By 1860, Singer had become the world's largest producer of sewing machines. In 1885, the company introduced its first electric-powered sewing machine.

New military designs appeared, including planes for bombing and aerial spy missions, submarines, and tanks. Designers created new weapons, such as deadly land mines, grenades, and machine guns. New designs improved field artillery, making it more accurate and deadly.

During World War II, many factories in the United States worked full-time producing goods for the war effort. The U.S. government established several top-secret research programs and facilities to develop and design weapons, technologies, and products, all aimed at winning the war. One of these facilities, the Los Alamos Scientific Laboratory near Santa Fe, New Mexico, developed and built the first atomic bomb.

A riveting team works on the cockpit shell of a C-47 transport at the plant of North American Aviation Inc. in Inglewood, California, 1942.

credit: Alfred T. Palmer, Office of War Information

alloy: a substance made of two or more metals or of a metal and a nonmetal that are united (usually by melting them together).

splint: a piece of rigid material used to keep a broken bone from moving after being set.

Government money flowed to manufacturers to spend on research and development. Using this funding, manufacturers created functional designs for military tools that performed better on the battlefield. Automobile companies, aircraft companies, and many civilian manufacturers all stopped production of consumer goods and devoted their factories to the production of military equipment, from tanks to radio antennas.

With government money, engineers and designers were able to speed up the development of many state-of-the-art materials, including plastics and metal **alloys**. They also developed new production techniques and technologies and built cutting-edge defense plants and factories to churn out needed military equipment.

After the war, the materials and technologies designed for military purposes could be used in the design of new consumer products. For example, bonding techniques developed for wartime aircraft manufacturing could be used to attach rubber shock mounts to a chair's plywood seat, back, and supporting frames. In the world of industrial design, repurposing and reusing are key!

DID YOU KNOW?

The materials and technologies developed during wartime had a significant effect on postwar industrial design, especially in the United States.

Many people received valuable, hands-on experience designing products for military use during the war. For example, industrial designers Charles Eames (1907–1978) and Ray Eames (1912–1988) designed molded plywood leg **splints** and stretchers for the U.S. Navy during the war. This experience provided the opportunity for experimenting with new materials and technologies and creating designs that solved real-world problems.

The United States emerged from World War II strong and confident in its industrial power. The factories that produced aircraft and other war materials were ready for the mass production of consumer goods.

ESSENTIAL QUESTION

Why did the world move from craft-based design to mass manufacturing?

Designer vs. Craftsman

The growth of factories and mass production allowed companies to produce goods that were affordable for many people. At the same time, separating design from manufacturing can cause some problems. In this activity, you will explore some of the differences between craft-based design and mass production.

❯ **To begin, you will play the role of a craftsperson.** Choose something that you can make, such as a piece of art, a stick picture frame, a simple wooden train and tracks, or a magnetic clip. Gather your supplies and get to work designing and making your item. Think about the following questions.

✱ What design decisions did you make for your item?

✱ When did you make these decisions—before you started working or while you were making the item?

✱ How were the design process and the making of the item connected? How were they separate?

❯ **Now, imagine that your item will be mass-produced in a factory.** You are still the designer, but will not be making the items. How will you convey your design ideas to the people who will manufacture and assemble the items? How will you ensure that the mass-produced items match your design, regardless of who makes them?

DID YOU KNOW?

Industrial designers work on consumer products such as hand tools, appliances, automobiles, and furniture, as well as on technical and professional products such as industrial vehicles, medical equipment, and computer hardware and software systems.

Activity continued on next page . . .

❯ **Have several friends or classmates follow your design instructions and make the item without you.** After they have finished, compare their items to your handcrafted original.

* Are there any differences? If so, what are they?

* What difficulties did you and your team encounter while mass-producing the item? Why do you think this occurred?

* What problems will it cause if there are differences between a design and the manufactured products? What about between the products themselves?

* What could you do as the designer to ensure there are very few differences between the original design and mass-produced items?

Try This!

Think about how ornamentation affects mass-produced industrial design. Ornamentation is everything added to an object for decoration. It could be the type of finish or painting on an object, scrolls in woodwork, or even added jewels or metalworking. What is the effect of ornamentation on an object's form, function, manufacturing process, and cost?

Chapter 2

THE **DESIGN PROCESS**

Have you ever wondered where the ideas for new products come from? New products don't just appear out of thin air. That cell phone you love or your baby sister's new favorite toy is the result of countless months of work.

ESSENTIAL QUESTION

How does having a checklist of design steps make for a better product?

A team of people—including **market researchers**, designers, engineers, marketing experts, and more—came together to create it. Long before a product hits the shelves in stores, the design team is working on it through the design process. Let's take a look at what the design process consists of.

GETTING STARTED: UNDERSTAND THE PROBLEM

Whether it's a toy, a chair, or a music player, industrial design is an attempt to solve a problem. Therefore, before any work on the design of a product can begin, the team needs to understand what the problem is. How do they do this? Through a lot of research! Through fact-finding missions and investigation, the team tries to answer the following questions.

- What is the problem or need?

- Who does the problem affect?

- Why is the problem important to solve?

The team gathers information from many different places. They talk to people who currently use or will be using the product. They ask users about their experiences, problems, and desires. What do users want? What are they using right now? Why is it not meeting their needs?

DID YOU KNOW?

If existing solutions do not meet user needs, understanding where they fall short can give the team valuable information about past mistakes.

The team observes users in their daily lives to better understand the problem and how it occurs in the real world.

Researchers gather information by studying **trends** and fashions. They talk to sales and marketing departments to learn what buyers want and get feedback on current products. The team also examines what others have done. What products or solutions already exist that solve similar problems? Team members check out the competition to see what products are already in stores and how well these products solve the problem.

DEFINE THE DESIGN REQUIREMENTS

Once the team members have defined the problem, they think about what needs to be included in a solution. **Design requirements** are the important characteristics a solution must have in order to be successful.

For example, imagine a poorly designed dog leash. These leashes fray easily and sometimes even break. They are also too short and difficult to use with multiple dogs. You decide that you want to design a better dog leash. From your research on dog leashes, you know that for a new dog leash to be a success, it must meet several design requirements and have the following characteristics.

- Be made of stronger and more **durable** material than the leashes that already exist
- Have an adjustable length
- Have an attachment to hook multiple dogs without tangling
- Be easily stored
- Cost the same or less than leashes currently on the market

Brainstorming Ideas

If you're feeling stuck and are having trouble generating new ideas, you can use several techniques to come up with design ideas. First, look at the existing solutions to your problem or similar problems. Studying these solutions might trigger your own creative ideas. How can a solution be improved? Can two solutions be combined to make a better one? By asking these questions and more, you might be able to generate some new concepts. For some people, sketching can spark new ideas and help them visually connect ideas. Even if the idea is not complete, a quick sketch can help people see possibilities that they had not considered.

Design requirements can involve any product characteristics, such as size, cost, materials, functionality, or ease of use. A design requirement is something that is necessary to solve the design problem. If it is not needed to solve the problem, the feature is not a requirement. Design requirements also have to be **feasible**. A dog leash made out of invisible thread might be really cool to imagine, but it's not really possible. If it can't be done, it's not a design requirement.

GENERATING PRODUCT IDEAS

After gathering information about the problem and design requirements, the design team generates product ideas to solve the design problem. Good designers try to brainstorm as many solutions as they can before picking the best one. Even an idea that seems crazy at first might have some features that make another idea better. The creative process of generating and developing new ideas is called **ideation**.

Group brainstorming sessions are a great way to generate a lot of possible ideas. In these sessions, team members get together to talk about what type of product should be developed. They might sit around a table and discuss each person's ideas. Designers need to be willing to think out of the box—no idea is too wild at this point! Even if the team members think they have a great solution from the start, they should brainstorm as many solutions as they can. You never know what new ideas might emerge from an original solution.

DID YOU KNOW?

One of the best ways to identify design requirements is to study similar products already in the market, analyzing how and why each works the way it does and noting key features.

CHOOSE THE BEST IDEA

Storyboard It!

Some design teams use **storyboards** during the development process. A storyboard is a series of graphic drawings or images. They allow a person to **visualize** a video, website, software program, user experience, and more. A storyboard shows how a user interacts with a product or an experience and breaks down the experience into its individual pieces, which allows the team to analyze each point more closely. This helps designers identify any problems that may appear in the flow of the experience. Typically, designers use storyboards during the early stages of product research, when creating a prototype, or when presenting a final product or solution.

Once the team has come up with a list of possible solutions to the design problem, members pick the best one (or ones) to develop. They look at each possible solution and see how it meets the design requirements. Solutions that do not meet all the requirements are rejected.

Of the remaining solutions, the team looks at the features of each. In addition to features that are part of the design requirements, some features are often nice to have. For example, a dog leash that converts to a car harness would be nice, but not required. Solutions that include some desirable, but not required, features might be better than others.

The design team also considers some **universal** design **criteria**. These criteria apply to almost every design.

• Elegance: Is the design simple or clever?

• Robustness: Is it sturdy and unlikely to break or fail?

• Aesthetics: Is it pleasing to look at?

• Cost: What will it cost? Can the company build it? Can typical users afford it?

• Resources: Do you have the materials and equipment needed to make it? If you don't, can you get them easily?

• Time: How long will it take to complete the design and get a product to market?

• Skills: Do you have the necessary skills to make the product?

• Safety: Is the product safe to make, use, store, and dispose of?

Designers consider all this information when deciding which design idea is best. Sometimes, the best solution is easy to identify. Other times, it's more difficult, especially when there are several good ideas. To help them decide, some designers will create a pro/con list for each possible solution. Others will compare solutions in a **decision matrix** that lists the design requirements and other criteria.

DEVELOP THE SOLUTION

Once the design team picks an idea, the next step is to develop it. The main goal of product development is to come up with a workable solution to the identified problem.

DID YOU KNOW? When brainstorming ideas, designers want to create a product that will be useful to customers and will also be a good fit for the company manufacturing it.

Designs can be developed in several ways. One of the most common techniques is sketching. A sketch is a quick and rough drawing, often done **freehand**, that shows a general outline of an idea. Sketching quickly puts an idea into a visual format that everyone can easily see. Designers use sketches to record ideas, communicate ideas to others, and study how different parts of a design work together.

Designers use several types of sketches and drawings during development. An idea sketch is rough and missing many details. Designers typically create an idea sketch when they are in the early stages of developing an idea.

Idea sketches are two-dimensional and are used to show how a design looks as a physical object.

In development, designers create additional sketches that **refine** the image and include more details about the product's appearance, **proportions**, **scale**, **layout**, and more.

Pictorial drawings create a photo-like representation of the design. **Technical drawings** show a product's actual size and shape and how its parts work together. These drawings include every detail needed to manufacture the product.

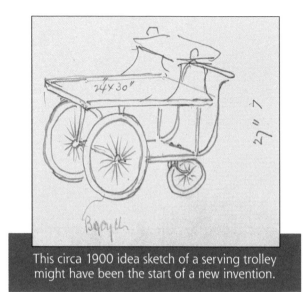

This circa 1900 idea sketch of a serving trolley might have been the start of a new invention.

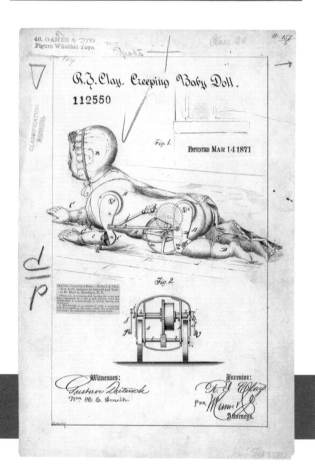

This 1871 idea sketch shows early designs for a very strange doll!
credit: U.S. National Archives

MAKE A MODEL

The next step in the development process is creating a model. Some models are physical objects. A **scale model** is a copy of an object that is usually smaller than the actual size of the object. Designers use a scale model to see how an object will look in real life. A scale model can also be used as a guide when building a full-size object.

For certain products, a design team might make a full-size model. Holding the three-dimensional (3-D) model in your hand or seeing a scale of its length, width, and height can help you get a good idea of whether or not you are on the right track. Some models are made of materials such as Styrofoam or are created by **3-D printers**. Using models, the design team can tweak the details of the product and make decisions about finish, color, and surfaces.

Other models are computer-generated. For complex or large objects, such as airplanes and spacecraft, using a computer-generated model can be less expensive and time-consuming than building a physical scale model. A computer-generated model can also help the designer identify areas in the design that need to be adjusted.

Does your school or library have a 3-D printer? These printers lay down layers of material to create 3-D objects, such as models and machine parts.

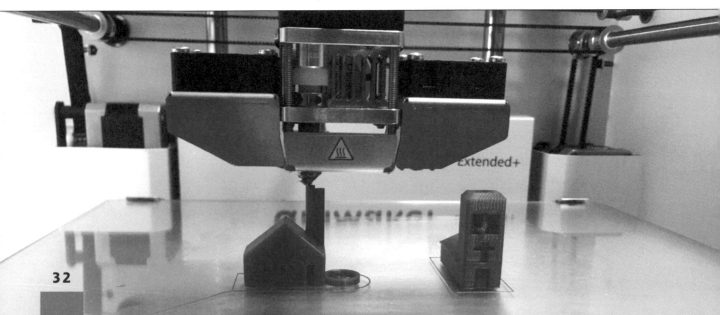

CREATE A PROTOTYPE

Once a design is complete, the design team creates a prototype of the product. A prototype is a working version of a product. It allows the design team to develop and test the structure, function, and appearance of the product.

A prototype might be built with different materials from the final product and is often not as polished as the final product. However, a prototype is an important step in the design process. The design team uses prototypes to test how the product will work. A prototype can be given to users to get their feedback about the product and its features.

Sometimes, the design team will make several prototypes during the design process, until the design is just right.

DID YOU KNOW?

When product testing, you can never have too many testers! The more people who test the product, the more information the team will gather to make the most successful product.

interaction: how things work together.

loop: a process that, upon reaching the end, returns to the beginning to start over.

TEST THE PRODUCT

Once the engineers have a prototype, they can begin one of the most important parts of the design process—product testing and redesign. Product testing involves using the product to see if it works as intended.

It's important to involve users in the testing process. They can provide valuable input on how the product works, what they like about it, and what needs improvement. For example, if you are testing a prototype of your new dog leash, you might want to recruit potential customers to test it—dog owners! You'll get the best feedback if you get a variety of dog owners to test the leash. People who own small dogs, large dogs, and multiple dogs can give you a variety of information when product testing. With many viewpoints, you can get the most complete feedback during product testing.

Users should also test the product in a real-world environment—test it the way they would use the product. For example, if you designed a new umbrella, you would have users test it on a rainy day. You wouldn't ask them to test the umbrella on a sunny day because that isn't how they would use the umbrella in the real world. Likewise, if your design is a website or software product, you would have users test it on a computer or smartphone.

When testing a new website, designers make sure to view it on different devices.

If the design is an experience or an environment, users should undergo the experience to test it. For example, a new soccer program might invite users to attend a test run of the program to give feedback on the fields, coaches, and more. By testing with real users in a real-world environment, the developers can gather the best information about how their program works.

When testing a design, the team should pay careful attention to the **interaction** between the user and the design. How do users experience the process or use the product? What do they do and how do they react? Do they appear confused at any point?

Noting the users' reactions can give the design team valuable information for any redesign.

The testing process often involves multiple **loops**. The team tests the product with users and identifies problems and hears suggestions for changes. Developers use these findings to make changes and redesign the product. Once redesign is complete, the team tests the redesigned product with users again. Even though it might seem tedious, this process of testing and redesign helps make the design the best it can be.

PRODUCT LAUNCH

Watch this product launch video for a water filter. Do you think this video is successful in driving interest in the product? What could the company have done better?

PS

🔎 Flowater Product video

Once the product design and development are complete, the product is ready for launch. The design team sends all of the design details to the manufacturing floor for production.

The design team also works with sales and marketing experts, who begin to make customers aware of the product and let them know what it is and how it works. Sales and marketing experts often use a variety of ways to get the word out about a new product, such as social media, websites, print advertisements, and email campaigns.

The design process involves a lot of people from design, engineering, marketing, and production working together to create a product that solves a problem.

In the next chapter, we'll take a look at some of the products that have emerged from this process. Many of them have changed the world!

ESSENTIAL QUESTION

How does having a checklist of design steps make for a better product?

A Design Checklist

Industrial designers consider several factors when creating a product.

> **Function:** Does the product show you what it does? Many industrial designers say that an object's form should inform users about its function.

> **Usability:** Does it work for the person who uses it? Designers study the age, size, strength, and interests of the people who want to use a product to make sure it works for them.

> **Ergonomics:** This is the science of designing and arranging things so that people use them efficiently and safely. Designers use ergonomics to make products safe, easy to use, and comfortable to use.

> **Aesthetics:** Designers select shapes, colors, and textures to make a product as appealing as possible to users. Sometimes, aesthetics change over time. For example, those plaid pants your grandfather wore in the 1970s are not that appealing today!

> **Green design:** Designers consider the effect their product has on the environment. Green designs use materials that are safe and renewable and consume less energy in their manufacture and in their use.

Identify a Problem

Industrial design results in a product that solves a problem. Designers take an existing problem, such as a chair that is uncomfortable or a fork that does not hold meat securely, and design a solution. What problem in your daily life might be solved by design?

❯ **Brainstorm a list of things that bother you or the people around you.** Write down everything! Challenge yourself to come up with as many ideas as you can and write them down in your design notebook. Here are some examples.

* Tangled headphone cords

* Nothing to hold your phone

* Mud in sneaker treads

* Computer keyboards that stick

❯ **Once you have a good list of potential problems, evaluate each one.** Which ones currently do not have a solution? Which ones have a solution that is not successful? Choose a problem you'd like to solve.

❯ **Once you've identified your problem, you'll need to define it.** Defining a problem is an important step designers take to make sure they design something that meets their goals. To define the problem, answer these questions.

* *What* is the problem?

* *Who* has the problem?

* *Why* is the problem important to solve?

❯ **Using the answers to these questions, you can create a problem statement, using the model,** WHO needs WHAT because WHY. For example, a problem statement might be: Kids need a way to store headphones easily because the cords are always getting tangled. What is your problem statement?

Try This!

Does everyone have the same problem with a product? You might think a chair is uncomfortable, while your friend thinks it is great. How does this difference affect how designers approach problem-solving in industrial design? Try creating another problem statement about a process instead of a product. Is it similar to your original problem statement? What's different about it?

Conduct Background Research

At the beginning of the design process, designers learn as much as they can about a problem and potential solutions by conducting background research. They study the experiences and mistakes of others so they can avoid making them! They investigate current solutions and competitors' products. They also talk to users about what they want and need.

Think about the problem you chose in the previous activity. How can you learn more about the problem and potential solutions?

❯ **To create a research plan, consider the following.**

* What do you want to know about the products that already exist to solve the problem or a similar problem? What are their strengths and weaknesses?

* Which users are interested in your solution or product? Why?

* What questions do you want to ask users or customers?

* What features do users consider very important?

* How can your design improve existing designs?

❯ **Now that you have a plan for what information you want to learn, go and gather it.** To conduct research, you can do the following.

* Observe users

* Research via the internet and library

* Examine and analyze similar products and solutions

❯ **Document your research** in your design notebook.

Consider This!

How can the information you learn during research change how you approach a new design? What type of information is most useful? Why? Did any of your research surprise you? What might a product be like if no research was done before the design stage? Do you think this product would be successful?

Brainstorm and Sketch a Solution

A good designer tries to come up with as many possible solutions as they can, then picks the one they believes is the best. The creative process of creating and developing ideas is called ideation. To generate ideas, designers study existing products and solutions. They brainstorm ideas, and some designers sketch and doodle possible ideas.

❯ **Take the problem that you identified in a previous activity** as something you want to solve. Go through the process of ideation and come up with as many possible solutions as you can. The process of ideation does not happen in a few minutes. In fact, it's often one of the longest parts of the design process. You don't need to find the perfect solution in one sitting. Come back to the problem the next day and see if you can come up with any new ideas.

❯ **Next, evaluate your potential solutions** and choose the best one to develop. Some solutions meet more requirements than others. If a solution does not meet enough of the design requirements, discard it.

❯ **Once you have chosen the best solution, develop your idea.** Start with a rough sketch of your idea. Then, add details and refine it with additional sketches. Include measurements and other details about the finished product. When finished, you should have a very detailed sketch that includes all of the information and features about your product design.

Try This!

Some designers use storyboards to show how a user will interact with a product during the development phase. Create a storyboard for your design idea. Does it help? How?

Check out a video about storyboarding! Notice that you need only stick figures to make a funny story.

🔎 Jefferson Media storyboard

Analyze and Determine Design Requirements

Design requirements are a critical part of industrial design. If a product does not meet the design requirements, it will not be successful. Therefore, identifying the features that are design requirements compared to those that are just "nice to have" is essential at the beginning of the design process.

❯ **Once you have a problem that you want to solve, what are the specific needs that must be met in order to solve the problem?** These are your design requirements. If you are designing a physical product, your problem is often making something easier for a user to do. Take your problem statement and start asking questions. Let's use the sample problem statement from the previous activity.

Problem Statement: Kids need a way to store headphones easily because the cords are always getting tangled.

What are the major needs and design requirements in this statement?

✱ Major need: Something to store headphones that helps the user

✱ Design requirement: Cords must not get tangled

❯ **For each need you identify, consider this question:** What is absolutely essential to satisfy the need?

❯ **Create a table in your design notebook** that lists the essential needs and the requirements necessary to meet those needs. These answers are design requirements because they must be part of the solution in order to meet the need and solve the problem.

❯ **What are the physical requirements of the product?** These answers can also be design requirements. For example, the physical requirements in our tangled headphone problem could be that it must be small enough to store on a desk or light enough to carry in a backpack.

> **What are the other requirements for your design solution?** Although these are not physical requirements, they must be met for a successful solution. These other requirements include cost and how long it will take to make the product.

> **What other products exist that serve a similar function to solving your problem?** For example, what other tools exist to store or untangle headphone cords? Research and examine these products and identify the components of each.

* What purpose does each component serve?

* Do you plan to have any features that are not in competing products?

* Do any of these components meet a need in your solution? If so, add it to your list of design requirements.

> **Are there any other essential features that should be included in your design requirements?** How are they essential to making your design successful?

> **Record all of your design requirements and research** in your design notebook.

Consider This!

Analyze your design requirements for a process instead of a product. How are they different? How are they similar?

Design!

You can see some current designs at this website.

If you click through individual designers, you'll find some early sketches and descriptions of the original concepts. Why do some designs change drastically from early sketches to final design? Are there any that stay basically the same through the entire process? How important do you think it is to have a clear vision of the final product when you're first starting to design?

Build and Test a Prototype

To make sure their design ideas look, feel, and work as intended, designers build a prototype of their design. A prototype is a working model of a design. It might be made with different materials than the finished product and may not be as refined. However, it allows the design team to test its design to see how it works and how users react to it.

❯ **To build a prototype of your design** from the previous activity, use easy-to-find materials such as cardboard, paper, poster board, foam board, tape, and glue. Look around your home or classroom for more materials.

❯ **Build a prototype of your design.** Remember, this is not the final product.

✱ Why did you choose the materials that you did?

✱ How is your prototype like the finished product?

✱ In what ways is it different?

❯ **Test your prototype.**

✱ How does it look and feel?

✱ How does it work?

✱ Does it meet the design requirements?

❯ **Revise the prototype and test the revised prototype with users.** Gather their feedback on the prototype and make any changes necessary to improve it. What do they like about it? What do they dislike? You may need to repeat this step several times.

Consider This!

Why is testing and redesign an extremely important step in the design process? What would have happened if you had not performed any testing and had gone straight into production with your product design?

Develop a Marketing Plan for Product Launch

Now it's time for the final step of the product design process—product launch! The purpose of a product launch is to build excitement and bring in customers and sales for a new product.

❯ **Develop a marketing plan** to sell the product you designed in a previous activity. The marketing plan should include the following elements.

✱ A written description of the product

✱ A written description of product testing and user feedback

✱ A selling proposition that identifies the qualities of your product that make it different from other products in the market. Qualities can include price, quality, size, color, or other characteristics.

✱ An explanation of what the product will do for users

✱ Identification of the target market, the people who want or need this product. How can you best reach this target market? Where do these potential customers go, what television shows do they watch, what magazines do they read, what websites do they visit?

✱ A detailed plan to market the product, including a sample advertisement

Try This!

Choose a new product in the market and learn what the company did to launch the product. Were these product launch activities successful? Why or why not? What should the company have done differently?

Chapter 3

HOW INDUSTRIAL DESIGN
CHANGED
THE WORLD

Industrial design has created some of the world's most well-known products. Have you ever used a toaster, flushed a toilet, or ridden an escalator? All these ordinary objects were created through industrial design! Each product solved a problem and created a better way to get something done.

There are many important products that we would have a hard time living without. Let's take a closer look at some of the design paths taken by products that ended up having a huge influence on the world.

ESSENTIAL QUESTION

What characteristics do many designers have in common?

THE FIRST FLUSH

Can you imagine not having an indoor toilet? That's the way it was for people a few centuries ago. Before indoor toilets, people dealt with expelling **waste** in many ways. Some people used an outhouse or simply went outside. Both methods had drawbacks—it probably wasn't very comfortable at night or when it was raining or cold!

In **medieval** England, people used **chamber pots**, which were small bowls they kept under the bed. Every day, they emptied the chamber pot, sometimes by throwing its contents out the window onto the street. This method was not so great for the people standing below the window! Some wealthy people used a **garderobe**, which was a room that stuck out over a moat. The room had an opening for waste so that it could fall into the water. In London, many used a large public garderobe that dumped its waste directly into the Thames River. All these methods were uncomfortable, smelly, and unsanitary.

The garderobe at Peveril Castle, Castleton, Derbyshire, England
credit: Dave.Dunford

WORDS TO KNOW

cistern: a tank for storing water.

sewer: a drain for wastewater.

sanitation: conditions relating to public health and cleanliness, especially clean drinking water and adequate sewage disposal.

contaminate: to pollute or make dirty.

commission: an instruction given to another person, such as an artist, for a piece of work.

ballcock: a valve that automatically fills a tank after liquid has been drawn from it.

conservation: preventing the overuse of a resource.

During the sixteenth century, Sir John Harington (1561–1612) of England designed an early toilet to solve some of these problems. Harington's design called for a deep oval bowl fed by several gallons of water from an upstairs **cistern**. He constructed a working model for his godmother, Queen Elizabeth I (1533–1603). However, it did not catch on with the public.

Two centuries later, Alexander Cumming (1731–1814), a watchmaker, developed the first successful flush toilet. His design used a separate water tank high above the seat. To flush it, people pulled on a chain. Cumming also developed the S-shaped pipe below the bowl, which created a seal and prevented smelly **sewer** gas from entering the room through the toilet.

As England's population increased during the nineteenth century, **sanitation** became a huge problem. Sewage from overcrowded public toilets spilled into the streets and rivers and **contaminated** the drinking water supply. Water-borne diseases such as cholera killed tens of thousands of people. To solve the problem, the British government declared that every new house should have a room with a flush toilet. They also **commissioned** the building of a London sewer system to dispose of the waste. As towns adopted the new toilets and sanitation systems, deaths from water-borne diseases dropped dramatically.

The construction of the great sewage tunnels, near old Ford, Bow, England. Wood engraving, nineteenth century
credit: Wellcome Collection. (CC BY 4.0)

Florence Knoll

Born in 1917 in Saginaw, Michigan, Florence Schust Knoll became one of the most influential designers in postwar America. Known as "Shu" to her family and friends, Knoll discovered her love of design in high school and studied architecture in college. After moving to New York City in 1941, she met Hans Knoll, a German furnituremaker who had come to America to build his modern furniture company, the Hans Knoll Furniture Co. Knoll became Hans's interiors specialist and later, his wife. Together, the pair grew the company, renamed Knoll Associates, and expanded its furniture lines.

Knoll established the Knoll Planning Unit, which researched and interviewed each client to determine their needs, define patterns of use in their office, and understand their company hierarchy, all before creating a comprehensive interior design. Knoll and the planning unit replaced traditional offices filled with heavy furniture with modern, lighter designs. She introduced the concepts of efficiency and space planning, creating office interiors for some of the country's largest corporations, including IBM, General Motors, and CBS. Knoll also designed furniture. After Hans Knoll's death in 1955, Knoll led the company for several years. In 1960, she resigned as president to become the director of design. In 1965, she retired from the company, leaving many contributions to modern corporate design.

Toilet designs continued to improve through the years. In the late nineteenth century, Thomas Crapper (1836–1910) manufactured the first successful line of flush toilets and created the **ballcock**, a tank-filling mechanism that is still used in modern toilets. Today, designers have improved the flush toilet, bringing the water tank down and making it part of the toilet. This makes the toilet easier to install and maintain. It also makes it more efficient. As water **conservation** has become a priority, modern designers have created efficient, low-flush toilets that prevent clogging.

Today's toilet designers research the best height, shape, and comfort features. Through design, the modern flush toilet has become the ideal place to go!

A TOAST TO DESIGN

"Want some toast with your scrambled eggs?" Today, it's easy to pop two slices of bread into an electric toaster. In a minute or two, perfectly toasted bread pops out. But toasting bread wasn't always so easy. Before the invention of the toaster, people had to spear a piece of bread with a fork and hold it over an open fire or a stove top. It was a tedious process that produced a lot of burnt toast.

In the early 1900s, an engineer named Albert Marsh (1877–1944) created a metal alloy of nickel and chromium, called **nichrome**. Marsh's alloy could be easily shaped into wires that conducted low amounts of electricity. Designers took this new material and used it to create electric toasters.

In 1909, General Electric (GE) introduced its electric toaster. The GE toaster was a wire skeleton with a rack for the bread. To make toast, people put a piece of bread on the rack facing heated electric coils. When one side was toasted, they turned the bread by hand. Although the GE toaster was a commercial success, it was not perfect. If people didn't turn the bread at the right time, the toast was underdone or overcooked. Additionally, the temperature of the toaster could not be controlled. These flaws led to more burnt toast.

Can you imagine making toast in this? How has the design of toasters changed?

General Electric Model D-12 toaster, 1910s. On exhibit in the National Museum of American History, Washington, DC

A decade later, a mechanic named Charles Strite (1878–1956) grew frustrated with the burnt toast served in his company cafeteria. He decided to solve the problem. How? By adding springs and a timer to the toaster's design. The timer turned off the heating element and released the spring, which caused the toast to pop up. In 1919, Strite patented his pop-up toaster, which he called the Toastmaster. By 1926, the Toastmaster was selling to the public. Sales picked up even more when the Continental Baking Co. introduced pre-sliced bread in 1930. Toasting bread had never been so easy.

Soon, the Toastmaster became a standard appliance in households across America.

Toasters have continued to evolve. Today's toaster uses **microchips** to program the toasting of a variety of baked goods, from bagels to English muffins. Designers have created models with wider openings for thick bagels and bread slices, as well as models that have as many as six slots for toasting a lot of bread at once. Can you think of more ways to make toasters even better?

SKATING BY DESIGN

Designs rarely stay the same. As time passes, form and functionality change when designers improve and add to their original ideas. Roller skates are one example of how designs changed.

For hundreds of years, people in Scandinavia used ice skates to travel across frozen canals and lakes. In the early 1700s, a Dutchman wanted to skate in the summer. He nailed wooden spools to pieces of wood and attached them to his shoes. It was the first pair of dry-land skates.

A young man wearing roller skates in 1910. How are these different from roller skates you might see worn today?
credit: George Grantham Bain Collection, Library of Congress

WORDS TO KNOW

maneuver: movements made with skill and care.

ball bearing: a part of a wheel that uses small metal balls to reduce friction between the wheel and a fixed axle.

friction: the resistance that one surface or object encounters when moving over another.

Around 1760, Belgian inventor Joseph Merlin (1735–1803) designed a pair of skates with small metal wheels. This solved the problem of wooden wheels not being very durable. In 1819, French inventor Monsieur Petibledin (dates unknown) further improved the design by making a skate that used four rollers attached to a wooden sole that fit on the bottom of a shoe.

Although the skates worked well for moving in a straight line, they were difficult to **maneuver**, and skaters were limited to making a few wide turns. To solve this problem, in 1863 American James Plimpton (1828–1911) designed a "rocking skate" that could turn. Plimpton's skate had four wheels, a pair in the front and a pair in the back. The wheels also had rubber springs, so a skater could move forward and backward, and turn. This type of skate design quickly became the standard used by manufacturers.

As time passed, designers made other changes to the roller skate's design. Early skates were heavy, and the wheels were hard to turn. In the 1880s, the use of pin **ball bearing** wheels made skates lighter. Ball bearings also reduce **friction**, which made the skate wheels turn faster and more smoothly.

Another problem was that skates were typically attached to a person's shoes with leather straps that broke frequently. Designer E.H. Barney (1835–1916) solved this problem by using a clamp that attached the skate to a shoe. It could be tightened with a key so that the skates did not fall off. Other designers created a skating boot with wheels attached to metal plates.

In the 1970s, plastic wheels became popular, which made skating smoother and easier. In the 1980s, brothers Scott (1960–) and Brennan Olson (1964–) of Minnesota wanted to adapt their hockey boots so they could cross-train in the summer. They found an old pair of roller skates that used in-line wheels instead of Plimpton's four-wheel design. Intrigued by the inline skates, the brothers decided to improve the design.

They took elements from the old inline skates and modern materials.

They created a skate that used four polyurethane wheels in a straight line attached to ice hockey boots. They called their skates "rollerblades" and in 1983 started a company called Rollerblade. The company mass-produced rollerblades and began selling them to the public.

The first mass-produced rollerblades had some flaws. They were hard to put on and to adjust. The wheels were easily damaged, and the brakes did not really work, which could be a problem. Also, the skates tended to collect dirt and moisture in the ball bearings. New designs solved these problems and introduced new materials and features.

Today, people around the world lace up a pair of inline skates and get moving. Some play inline hockey, while others skate for fun. Every year, designers refine the skates, improving comfort, durability, and performance to make them better than ever before!

WORDS TO KNOW

terracotta: earthen clay used as a material for buildings, pottery, and sculpture.

alabaster: a soft mineral or rock that is often carved.

fossil fuel: a natural fuel, such as coal, oil, or gas, formed during many years from the remains of living things.

flammable: easily set on fire.

carbonized: coated with carbon.

filament: a very fine wire or thread.

A BRIGHT IDEA

Long ago, the sun was the main source of light. People had to get all their work done during daylight hours before the darkness of night. With the discovery of fire, early people had torches to provide some light at night. While this solution was better than nothing, they needed a smaller, more controllable source of light.

One solution was the early oil lamp. People used shells, hollow rocks, or any material that would not burn. They soaked moss in animal fat and lit it to produce a flame.

As centuries passed, the materials used to make oil lamps improved. In ancient Egypt, Greece, and Rome, lamp makers made oil lamps from **terracotta**, bronze, stone, and **alabaster**. Designers changed the lamp's shape, so that the oil it held burned longer. The ancient Romans also developed some of the first wicked candles made by dipping rolled papyrus in melted animal fat or beeswax.

Lamps had several advantages over other lighting solutions. They were easier and safer to carry than torches with open flames. Unlike candles, they were reusable. People filled the lamps with olive oil or animal fat. They used a fiber wick to light the oil and create a flame. Today, some people still use oil lamps, but they mainly use paraffin or kerosene as fuel.

Damsels of Design

In the 1950s, few women worked in industrial design. Harley J. Earl (1893–1969), the vice president of General Motors (GM) Design believed female designers could help make cars that appealed to female buyers. In the mid-1950s, he recruited and hired several female designers. The group of 10 women, known as the "Damsels of Design," worked on the design of almost every part of the car's interior, including seats, doors, trim, color, fabric, and detailing for several GM brands. They added features that are still used in cars today, such as childproof door locks, lighted makeup mirrors, retractable seat belts, and storage consoles.

In the late 1700s, people discovered that they could burn other **fossil fuels**, such as gas from petroleum and coal. Designers created new solutions for lighting using these fuels. Gas lamps became popular in homes and outdoors. Yet, gas was poisonous and highly **flammable**—not the kind of material you want in your home.

Then, in 1879, American inventor Thomas Edison (1847–1931) came along with a bright idea. Fascinated by electricity, Edison was consumed by the idea of electric lighting. He believed that electric lighting was much safer than gas lights. Light bulbs had already been designed, but they weren't useful. They were large and they used lots of electricity. Several designers were already hard at work trying to create a better electric light bulb, but no one had been able to make one that burned for more than a few minutes.

For longer than a year, Edison searched for the right design for an electric light bulb. He built several models, but they all failed. His big breakthrough came when he discovered that a piece of **carbonized** cotton thread could be used as a **filament** that burned for several hours. Soon, Edison improved his filament so that it lasted for much longer.

Edison also helped design electrical systems that could provide power for people's homes and light his electric light bulbs.

The electric age had arrived. Edison's manufacturing company, the Edison Electric Light Co. made lights bulbs and parts for electrical systems. Within a few years, people across America were using Edison's electric light bulb. Innovation triumphed over the dark.

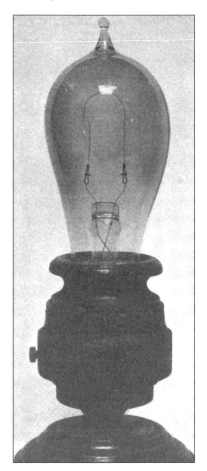

One of Edison's first carbon filament light bulbs

brittleness: easily damaged or broken.

purify: to make something clean and pure.

byproduct: a secondary product made in the manufacture of something else.

iconic: a widely recognized symbol of a certain time.

veneer: a thin decorative covering of fine wood.

ottoman: a low, upholstered footstool.

A TUPPERWARE PARTY

In the early 1940s, American inventor Earl Tupper (1907–1983) designed a new type of plastic storage container. He called the container Tupperware. Tupper owned a plastics manufacturing company in Leominster, Massachusetts. During World War II, Tupper's company produced military products such as gas masks and signaling lamps.

After the war, Tupper became interested in designing plastic consumer products such as sandwich picks and cigarette cases. In the 1940s, plastics had several drawbacks, including **brittleness**, odor, and greasiness. To create a better plastic, Tupper experimented with a **purified byproduct** of the oil-refining process. He created a plastic that was durable, flexible, odor-free, non-toxic, and lightweight.

Tupper planned to use his plastic to create food storage containers. He believed these could be used to keep food fresh in the new gas and electric refrigerators that were appearing in homes around the country. He designed a line of plastic containers that were lighter and less likely to break than traditional glass and stone food containers. He also designed and patented the Tupper Seal, an airtight and watertight lid, modeled after the design of a paint can lid.

DID YOU KNOW?

Is there any Tupperware in your kitchen? You can still host a Tupperware party today!

However, Tupper's containers did not sell well in retail stores. No one could figure out how they worked.

To solve this problem, the company introduced the Tupperware Home Party. The first party was held in 1948, and it provided a new way for Tupperware to reach consumers. Independent party hostesses demonstrated the product and talked about the benefits of the airtight seal. People then placed their orders for the product.

Tupperware parties soon became as famous as its plastic products. Together with the refrigerator, Tupper's design allowed food to be stored longer, kept fresh longer, and stacked neatly. This is a great example of both innovative product design and innovative marketing!

AMERICA'S FAVORITE CHAIR

The Eames lounge chair is one of the most **iconic** chairs ever made. Charles Eames (1907–1978) and Ray Eames (1912–1988) were an American husband-and-wife design team. Their goal was to create stylish designs that could be cheaply mass-produced.

In the 1950s, Charles and Ray began designing a high-end, luxury chair. It needed to be modern and stylish. It also had to be comfortable. In the early design stages, the couple imagined a person nestled in a worn and broken-in leather baseball glove. They wanted a person sitting in their chair to feel snug and cozy, as if wrapped in warm leather. This vision led to the idea for the Eames Lounge Chair.

You can watch a 1956 *Today Show* television interview with Ray and Charles Eames at this website. What differences do you notice about this interview compared with one that might be aired today?

PS

🔍 Today Show Eames

To build the chair, Charles and Ray used three pieces of molded plywood which formed the chair's base, backrest, and headrest. They covered each piece with a rosewood **veneer**. Then, they added leather cushions. To finish the chair, they designed a matching **ottoman**.

An authentic Eames chair
credit: David Costa (CC BY 2.0)

The Herman Miller Co. started to sell the Eames Lounge Chair in 1956. This chair became the first luxury furniture item to be made with plywood and designed for mass production.

The Eames Lounge Chair was an enormous commercial success. Decades later, the chair is still produced and sold. The chair's smooth design became the standard for other furniture designers.

These designs and designers are just a few examples of the role industrial design has played in changing the world.

From the toilet to Tupperware, the products came about because their designers identified a problem, rolled up their sleeves and found a solution, tested it, and brought it to the world. Because of these iconic designs, the world has become a much more interesting place!

DID YOU KNOW?

The original Eames Lounge Chair can be seen at the Museum of Modern Art in New York and the Museum of Fine Arts in Boston, Massachusetts.

ESSENTIAL QUESTION

What characteristics do many designers have in common?

Research an Iconic Design

How often do you think about the design of the objects you use every day? Iconic designs are all around us, from a ballpoint pen to a Chinese food container. Let's take a deeper look.

❯ **Choose an object that interests you to learn more about its design.** Some objects to consider researching include:

* Swingline stapler
* Polaroid camera
* Q-tip
* Flat-bottom paper bag
* Post-it Notes

* Soy sauce bottle
* Nike "swoosh"
* Glass Coke bottle
* Lego brick

DID YOU KNOW?

You can read about some of the most well-known designs at this website.

🔎 complex iconic designs

❯ **Using resources from the library or the internet, research the details of your chosen object and its design story.** Consider the following questions in your research.

* Who designed the object?
* What problem was the object intended to solve?
* What were the object's design requirements?

* Does the object do everything it needs to do?
* Does it look good?
* Does it solve the problem it was intended to solve? Why or why not?

❯ **Using the results of your research,** create a PowerPoint presentation to share the design story.

Consider This!

Can you think of any improvements that could be made to the design of this object? Explain.

Design a Chair

Design solves a problem and meets a need. When industrial designers create and improve products, they make sure their designs meet the needs of users. In this activity, you'll design a chair that meets the needs of a specific type of user.

▶ **Consider the following chair users.**

* An 80-year-old man who walks with a cane. He spends most of his day in a chair, watching television. It is difficult for him to get in and out of a chair.

* A 15-year-old student who spends eight hours a day at school. He has a large, heavy backpack that he carries from class to class. In every class, he needs a place to work and store his backpack.

* A 30-year-old marathon runner who spends much of her time moving. Because she often has sore muscles, she prefers a cushioned, comfortable place to relax and prepare for the next day's run.

▶ **Choose one of the users and make a list of what they need in a chair.** How are these needs related to design requirements for a chair?

▶ **Choose a variety of materials to work with.** Possibilities include black permanent markers, paper, scissors, corrugated cardboard, pipe cleaners, modeling clay, cotton balls, tape, and toothpicks.

▶ **Following the design process and considering your design requirements, design the chair.**

* Draw several sketches of the design. What elements will you use in the design? How do these elements meet design requirements?

* Using your materials, make a simple model of your chair.

* Evaluate your chair's design. Does it meet the design requirements? Does it work as intended? Is it aesthetically pleasing?

* Test your design by having other people evaluate the chair. What changes or improvements do they recommend?

> **Retest it with potential users.** If needed, redesign your chair based on the testing feedback. After you have the final design, consider the following questions.

✳ What did you change during the design process? What did you learn from your models and prototypes?

✳ What materials did you enjoy working with the most? Which did you enjoy the least? Why?

Try This!

Try building a model of the same chair using different materials. How do different materials affect the design? How does the choice of materials affect how well the chair meets the design requirements?

A Design Change: Green Lighting

In the 1970s, during what was called the Arab oil embargo, the United States experienced oil shortages and significant increases in the price of oil. This experience marked the beginning of a movement toward energy efficiency and conservation. Congress established the U.S. Department of Energy in 1977 to **diversify** energy resources and promote energy conservation. As a result, a new design requirement emerged for many products that consumed energy: energy efficiency. Lighting technology is one area that has changed with the development of more **energy-efficient** products.

❯ **Consider the different light bulbs available today:**

* Incandescent

* Halogen

* Fluorescent

* Compact fluorescent (CFL)

* Light-emitting diode (LED)

❯ **What are the pros and cons of each?** Do some research online or at the library. Create a chart to compare each type of bulb.

* How do they compare in efficiency, light produced, average life, general aesthetics, ability to be dimmed, and cost?

* How does each meet green design requirements?

* Did adding a green design requirement affect the bulb's ability to meet other requirements, such as cost and aesthetics?

Try This!

What type of light bulbs do you use in your house? Check all the places you have light bulbs in your house. What changes can you make to the light bulbs you have to make your home more energy efficient and still meet your family's design requirements?

WORDS TO KNOW

diversify: becoming more varied.

energy efficient: using less energy to provide the same results.

Generate Ideas with Mind Mapping

Mind mapping is one technique that people use to brainstorm and generate ideas. A mind map is a diagram that links words, concepts, objects, or tasks to a central idea or subject. It is an easy way to brainstorm without worrying about order and structure.

❯ **To start, get a large piece of paper and several different-colored pens or pencils.** In the center of the paper, describe the problem to be solved by industrial design in one to three words. Circle it.

❯ **Next, think of words that are related to your original word or idea.** Write these words on the paper around the original word. Circle them and draw a line from their circle to the original circle. Keep adding words until you can't think of any more.

❯ **Once you've run out of words that connect to the original circle,** repeat the process for each circle in your second group of circles. Repeat until the paper is filled. Remember that the goal of mind mapping is to generate as many words and ideas as possible within a short period of time.

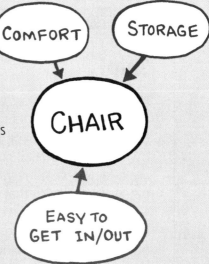

❯ **Review the words and ideas that you generated.** Does the process of mind mapping help you come up with a design solution to your problem? Do you feel comfortable with this method of brainstorming?

Try This!

Investigate other brainstorming techniques. Which one works the best for you?

Learn about an Icon of Industrial Design

Throughout history, several talented designers have contributed significantly to the field of industrial design. These men and women have created some of the world's most well-known products. They have incorporated form, function, and aesthetics to create products loved by users.

You can read about some of these designers at these websites.

🔍 Slate industrial designer

🔍 Ranker industrial designer

🔍 Auburn industrial designer

Snip!

How often do you cut your fingernails? It's a tedious chore that almost everyone shares, made slightly easier by modern fingernail cutters. These are a fairly recent invention. The first patent for a device that resembles what we use today was issued in 1881 to Eugene Heim and Oelestin Matz. Check out their original sketches. Do these look familiar to you? Can you spot any improvements that have been made since these were patented? How might people have clipped their nails before this invention? Do some research to find out! Hint: It wasn't easy.

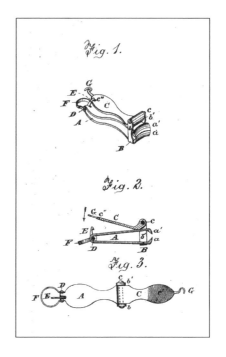

Activity

▶ **Choose a designer who you want to learn more about.** You can choose one of the following or someone else who interests you:

* Peter Behrens
* Dieter Rams
* Charlotte Perriand
* Raymond Loewy
* Henry Dreyfuss
* Zaha Hadid
* Russel Wright

* Charles and Ray Eames
* Jonathan Ive
* Bertha Benz
* James Dyson
* Adam Savage
* Ron Arad

▶ **Use the internet and library to research your chosen designer** and their design story. Think about the following questions.

* What is the designer's background? Where did they go to school? Where did they work?

* How did the designer get involved in design?

* What product(s) is the designer famous for designing?

* What problem(s) did the designer solve with their design?

* What or who influenced the designer?

* What successes and failures did the designer have in their career?

* What elements of design does the designer emphasize? What are they known for in design?

* How did this designer impact industrial design overall?

▶ **Using the information you learn, create a presentation** to share the designer's story.

Try This!

Choose a product that you use in your daily life. Who designed it? What is their design story?

The Meaning of Color

Color is an important part of a design. Color can influence how a person feels about a product. It can generate different emotions, associations, and responses that affect how a user views a product. Color also has different cultural meanings. For example, in some cultures, black is the color of death. In other cultures, white is the color of death. When choosing color, designers must be very careful!

❯ **Using the internet or a library**, investigate the emotional meaning of the following colors:

* Red
* Yellow
* White
* Black
* Silver
* Pink

* Blue
* Green
* Pastel colors
* Bright colors
* Dark colors

❯ **What types of products would be a good fit for each color?** What products would not be a good fit for a color? How does the choice of color in a design affect the user's decision to buy the product?

DID YOU KNOW?

How do you know that the blue you see on your computer screen will look like the same blue that gets printed on the newsletter you're designing? By using the Pantone Matching System (PMS). This is a numbering system for colors, so when a designer asks for Pantone 7459 C, a printer knows exactly what shade of blue they want.

Consider This!

Sometimes, designers use fancy names to describe colors to users. What is the difference between a bike painted a generic "red" or a fancier "candy apple red"? How does each color name make you feel? Find some examples online or in a store of different types of color names. Are they simple or fancy? Why do you think the company chose that type of color name? Can you think of some new color names?

Redesign a Kitchen Utensil

There are a lot of utensils in the kitchen—knives, forks, spoons, whisks, peelers, pizza cutters, ice cream scoopers, spatulas, and more. Can you find any that could be improved by industrial design?

❯ With an adult's permission, take an inventory of your kitchen utensils. Consider the following questions.

- **✱** What types of utensils do you have? How many of each kind?
- **✱** What materials are they made from?
- **✱** Are they ergonomic?
- **✱** Are any utensils hard to hold or difficult to use?
- **✱** Are any broken or rusty?

- **✱** Can you use them right-handed or left-handed?
- **✱** Do the handles wobble and make gripping the utensil difficult?
- **✱** Does the utensil have sharp edges that cut into your hand when holding?
- **✱** Do they look aesthetically pleasing?

❯ Choose a utensil to improve through industrial design. Follow the steps of the design process:

- **✱** Understand the problem
- **✱** Define design requirements
- **✱** Generate ideas
- **✱** Choose the best solution

- **✱** Develop the solution
- **✱** Make a model/build prototype
- **✱** Test and redesign

❯ Present your new and improved utensil design to family members. What are their reactions?

Try This!

Can you design a product to organize your kitchen utensils?

Chapter 4

INDUSTRIAL
DESIGN AND ELECTRONICS

Every year, new, high-tech devices are unveiled at consumer electronics shows. These devices promise to make our lives easier, more connected, and more fun. From laptops and tablets to smartphones and televisions, today's high-end electronics demonstrate cutting-edge engineering and design solutions.

The consumer electronics industry is constantly evolving to improve our lives. However, the product life for consumer electronics is often very short. Only a few months after the unveiling of a new design, the hardware and software are outdated, the design is stale, and something else has become the new must-have gadget.

ESSENTIAL QUESTION

How does the design of an electronic device affect the success of that device?

Since its beginnings, the story of consumer electronics and design has been about change. Let's take a look at some of the devices that have undergone major alterations since their inception.

VIDEO RECORDING IN THE ELECTRONICS AGE

In 1971, Sony introduced its first video cassette recorder (VCR). The technology behind the VCR had actually emerged years earlier. In the 1950s, televisions became increasingly popular in living rooms around the country. Typically, television networks broadcast news programs live from their studios. However, in a country such as the United States, with multiple time zones, live broadcasts posed a problem. A news broadcast in New York City that aired live at 6 p.m. on the East Coast would appear on television at 3 p.m. in San Francisco, California, when most people were still at work or in school.

What Is Electricity?

We all know that you need electricity to turn on the lights and power the television. But where does electricity come from? Electricity comes from electrons. An **electron** is a tiny **charged** part of an **atom**, the tiny particles that make up all matter. Electrons have a negative charge. When a force is applied, some electrons on the outside of an atom can come loose and move to another atom. When the electrons move from one atom to another in the same direction, this flow of electrons is called electricity.

WORDS TO KNOW

kinescope: a process that uses a special motion picture camera to photograph a television monitor.

magnetic tape: a medium for magnetic recording, made of a thin, magnetizable coating on a long, narrow strip of plastic film.

audio: relating to sound.

At the time, the only method of recording video footage and airing it later was by using **kinescope**, a process in which a special motion picture camera photographed a television monitor. It took hours to develop the kinescope film, and it made a poor-quality broadcast.

As a result, television networks had to choose between creating a second live broadcast for San Francisco or rushing to develop the kinescope film of the New York broadcast so that it could air on time in California.

The networks desperately needed a better recording technology.

Several electronic companies rushed to develop a new technology. Many experimented with video recorders that used **magnetic tape**. One company, called the Ampex Corp., worked on a solution that used a rotating head design—this had been used in **audio** recordings. In April 1956, Ampex released the world's first magnetic tape video recorder, the VRX-1000.

DID YOU KNOW?

The first use of color in a television broadcast aired during the Tournament of Roses parade in 1954. Color wasn't widely adopted in the United States until 1955.

You can see the two different recording techniques used for *The Edsel Show* in 1957. What do you notice about the kinescope technique vs. the video recorder? How do these images compare to the ones you might see today when streaming a movie on an electronic device?

🔎 Edsel CBS 1957 video

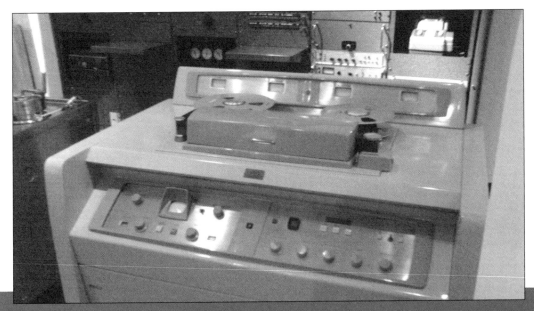

The first video recorder, 1950s. That's a lot larger than video recorders today!
creit: Karl Baron (CC BY 2.0)

While the technology was revolutionary, at a price of $50,000 per unit, it was also very expensive! Even so, the television networks raced to order the new video recorder. CBS was the first network to put the technology use. The network aired *Douglas Edwards and the News* on November 30, 1956, from New York. It recorded the broadcast and replayed it a few hours later on the West Coast. News anchor Edwards never had to repeat a live broadcast again.

Following Ampex's successful solution, other electronics companies also began to experiment with rotating head designs for video recording technology. The VRX-1000 was not suited to home use—it was too expensive and too complicated for the average user to operate. So, electronics designers attempted to develop a video recording machine for the home. Among the design requirements, the device had to be solid, easy to operate, and inexpensive.

Eventually, three VCR formats emerged: Sony's Betamax in 1975, JVC's VHS in 1976, and the Philips V2000 in 1978. The different formats did not work with each other. A video tape cassette that played on one machine would not play on another machine.

When Sony released its Betamax video recorder, company executives believed their technology and design were superior to anything else in the market. They believed other companies would abandon their research and design attempts and adopt Betamax as the industry-wide standard format.

However, JVC refused to adopt Betamax and introduced its own VHS format to the market a year later. Philips' V2000 soon followed, but because of technical problems, it never fully took off.

Who Designs What?

Electronic products such as computers, cell phones, and iPods have both hardware and software components. Who designs what part? Generally, industrial designers design the hardware, which includes the case that you see. Electronic and software engineers develop the software that makes the device work.

A VCR has a lot of different components

How Do Electric Circuits Work?

Electronic gadgets, from your iPod to your digital calculator, use energy in the form of electricity. To make electricity, we create an electric **circuit**. When you turn on a light in your house, you complete the electric circuit and cause electrons to move and electricity to flow through the light bulb, causing it to light. These are the main parts of an electric circuit.

> › **Power source:** a battery or a wall outlet. The flow of electricity starts and stops here.

> › **Conductor:** the wires that carry electricity. A **conductor** can be any material that allows electrons to flow.

> › **Load:** the device, such as a light bulb, that uses electricity

> › **Switch:** when closed, the switch connects the circuit and electricity flows. When open, the switch breaks the circuit and electricity cannot flow.

In an electrical circuit, a power source generates the force to move electrons through the conductors and into the load. A closed circuit is a complete circuit without gaps, while an open circuit has a gap or switch that is raised, which prevents the electrons from flowing.

For several years, Sony and JVC battled to win consumers. Whichever format they chose, consumers could now record television programs and watch them whenever they wanted. They could also buy or rent videos. While pretty basic compared to today's standards, the VCR was the first step toward personalized entertainment systems.

So, who won the format war? Although a better quality, Betamax machines were more expensive and harder to repair. Early models worked only with certain television sets. Video rental shops decided to make more VHS machines and VHS videos available for rent. Eventually, JVC's VHS edged Betamax out of the market.

Even then, technology and design did not stand still. In the late 1990s, the **DVD** player was introduced. A DVD is a type of compact disc that can store large amounts of data, making it ideal for videos. By 2003, DVD sales surpassed those of the VHS cassettes. Video rental shops began stocking DVDs instead of VHS cassettes.

And the change continues today, as digital video recorders and other new technologies offer consumers even more options for recording and replaying video. How do these changes in technology affect your day-to-day life? How do you watch movies and television shows at your house? What do you think the next step in recording might be?

EARLY DESIGNS IN GAMING

Do you know what the first video game was? You might have answered Pong, the ping-pong arcade game released by Atari in 1972. However, several months earlier, American electronics company Magnavox demonstrated and released the Magnavox Odyssey, the first home video game system.

The Odyssey was based on the Brown Box, a prototype designed by engineer Ralph Baer (1922–2014). Compared to today's video games, the Odyssey was downright primitive! It displayed only a few small, white blocks and a vertical line on the screen. It came with several games, including Table Tennis, which was similar to Pong. Users could place **translucent** color overlays on the screen to provide settings and layouts for different games. The Odyssey also came with a pack of non-electronic game accessories, including dice, a deck of cards, play money, and poker chips.

Although it was revolutionary in home gaming electronics, the Magnavox Odyssey was not a commercial success. Many people mistakenly believed that the game system would work only on Magnavox television sets. Only about 350,000 units were sold, a small number compared to the popularity of Atari's Pong.

You can still play Pong! **Give it a try at this site.**

🔍 play Pong

In 1977, the gaming industry took a giant step forward with the Atari 2600. Instead of being programmed with a set number of games, the Atari **console** could be used to play an unlimited number of game cartridges.

The release of the popular Space Invaders game for home use in 1980 sent sales of the Atari 2600 skyrocketing.

The development of video gaming included more than the design of a physical console. It also involved the design of the games. This widened the scope of electronics design and involved more software programming. Traditionally, designers created physical objects. Now, they were also creating objects, landscapes, characters, and plots in the digital world.

DID YOU KNOW?

American engineer Ralph Baer, who designed the Brown Box prototype that led to the Magnavox Odyssey, is known as the father of video games.

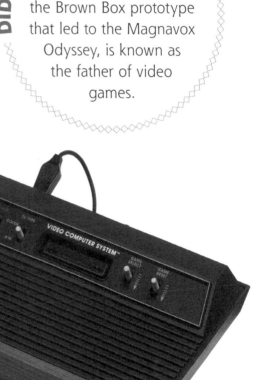

An Atari console from the early 1980s

revenue: money made by a business from selling products or services.

third-party developer: a company that develops software or games for another company's system.

surplus: more than what is needed.

THE DESIGN THAT SAVED GAMING

Between 1978 and 1983, the video game industry soared in popularity. **Revenues** peaked at around $3.2 billion in 1983. Then, the market crashed, falling to about $100 million in 1985. While many factors contributed to the crash, a major problem was an increase in consoles and video games that were produced in a rush and not well tested—these flooded the market.

Companies that saw the success of the Atari 2600 wanted in on the industry. **Third-party developers** flooded the market with their games, which were often of poor quality. Left with a **surplus** of unsold consoles and low-quality games, stores either returned them to the manufacturers or slashed prices. The industry crash caused several developers and console manufacturers to go out of business or abandon the video game market entirely. News reports declared the gaming fad over.

A New Type of Controller

The original Nintendo Entertainment System (NES) controller changed the way people interacted with video games. Earlier video games typically used complicated, difficult-to-use controllers. The NES controller's simple rectangular shape was ergonomically designed and more comfortable to use. Players used their thumbs to press the face buttons quickly. With increased functionality, the NES controller also allowed developers to design more sophisticated games. "Select" and "Start" buttons allowed game designers to add sub-menus where players could choose new abilities, objects, and more. While the design of game controllers has changed through the years, many still use the Nintendo's basic design.

Fortunately, the design that would revive the industry was already in the process of being developed. Thousands of miles away in Japan, industrial design was at work.

Seeing Atari's early success in America, another Japanese company, Nintendo, wondered if it could design something even better. Nintendo already had experience in gaming, making a popular line of arcade and dedicated home console games in Japan. Nintendo engineer Masayuki Uemura (1943–) was given the task of designing a console based on interchangeable game cartridges. He was inspired by Nintendo's popular line of Game & Watch handheld consoles.

When Nintendo released a multi-screen version of Game & Watch, Uemura realized that gamers were comfortable looking up at a second screen, instead of down at their hands while they played.

He also noticed that gamers liked the directional pad controller. He used both of these design elements in his development of the Family Computer, or the Famicom. Nintendo released the Famicom in Japan in 1983. By the end of 1984, it had become Japan's best-selling game console. Nintendo then turned its attention to the market in the United States.

A 1985 Nintendo game console

WORDS TO KNOW

peripheral: an accessory designed to work with a main video game console or computer.

accessory: something added to something else to make it more useful or add features.

licensed: granted permission to do something.

At the time, the American video game market was crashing. Stores were hesitant to stock a new gaming console that they might have a hard time selling. Nintendo and Uemura decided to make some design changes and positioned the Famicom as an electronic toy or entertainment system, instead of simply another video game console.

To do this, they made some changes to the console's design. Because the top-loading Famicom looked too much like a game console, they changed it to a front-loading design, inspired by the front-loading design of VCRs. This allowed it to be placed more easily on a TV stand with other entertainment devices, such as a VCR. Nintendo also developed a **peripheral** known as R.O.B. the Robot, an **accessory** that could be used with two games, and that made the NES more like an electronic toy.

They changed its name, selling it as the Nintendo Entertainment System (NES) to differentiate it from other game consoles at the time.

Nintendo also learned from Atari's mistakes with games. When launched, the NES had a strong, 18-game library. Nintendo also carefully reviewed and controlled the number of games that third-party developers could release for its console each year.

Third-parties, which had to be **licensed** to develop games for Nintendo's system, could release only two games a year. This ensured the market would not be flooded with low-quality games.

Learn more about the Famicon and see it played in this video. Do the video games you play today look different?

(PS)

Famicom video history

DID YOU KNOW?

On August 14, 1995, Nintendo discontinued the NES in both North America and Europe.

Video Game Designer

While some designers develop the hardware for video gaming consoles, other designers create the games themselves. Video game designers are responsible for the content and environment of a video game. At the beginning of the design process, designers write detailed descriptions of their ideas. They plan every aspect of the game, from plot and characters to game play. Not only do they brainstorm story lines, they must also account for every possible interaction or move a player may make in the game. Design teams meet regularly to review new game ideas and select the best ones to develop. Once a game idea has been selected for development, video game designers work closely with computer programmers and artists to make sure their ideas are being accurately translated into code and art.

When Nintendo launched the NES in the United States in 1985, it had redesigned the console and **rebranded** the product for the American audience. Nintendo tried to show Americans that the NES was something new and different from the disappointing video game consoles of recent years.

And they succeeded. For several years, the NES was the leading gaming console in the United States. This made Nintendo a major force in the gaming industry. Have you ever played on a Nintendo system?

APPLE'S IMAC

In the 1980s, many computer manufacturers—led by IBM—adopted a neutral beige color and plain design for their products. Beige was supposed to reduce user eye strain. By the mid-1980s, the millions of personal computers in homes across America looked almost the same—a rectangular beige box, a bulky beige monitor, a beige keyboard, and a beige mouse. Although the technology housed inside the computer improved, the outside remained the same.

An iMac G3 and an iBook
credit: Michael Gorzka

In August 1998, Apple launched the iMac G3, a brightly colored, translucent computer. In a sea of beige, the iMac was something completely different.

To start, it was an all-in-one design that combined the monitor, processor, and hard drive in a single, teardrop shape with a handle on top. The semi-translucent plastic body offered a glimpse of the computer's inner workings. A semi-transparent keyboard and mouse completed the set. At the time, Apple CEO Steve Jobs said the iMac looked like it was from another planet.

Technically, the iMac was not very different from other computers of the time. What set it apart, however, was that it was designed to be an internet computer. All iMacs came with a built-in telephone modem, which was used to access the internet. Other computers offered this feature only as an extra.

By the end of 1998, the iMac had become Apple's fastest-selling computer ever. While the iMac did little to change how people used computers, its design had a larger effect. It destroyed the myth that computers had to look dull and boring. Competitors rushed to develop their own computers with softer shapes and colors.

DID YOU KNOW?

Today's Apple iMac, in its seventh generation, consumes up to 96 percent less energy in sleep mode than the first iMac.

Apple responded by offering the iMac in five colors: pink, light green, purple, orange, and light blue.

With the iMac, Apple regained its position as the leading manufacturer of consumer computer products. It also opened the door for the development and release of new Apple products that all used the iMac as a hub, such as the iPod in 2001, the iPhone in 2007, and the iPad in 2010. For Apple, the iMac was an enormous success. Jonathan Ive's design for the iMac marked the point when computers stopped being just a tool to get work done and became a fashionable and desired device.

Consumer electronic products have changed the way people communicate, share information, and watch or listen to entertainment. Industrial design has been an integral part of bringing these products into our lives. The future will bring more changes with the advent and design of new technologies in smart homes, smart cars, and smartphones. For the designers who create these products, the future of electronics design is an exciting place to be.

ESSENTIAL QUESTION

How does the design of an electronic device affect the success of that device?

Then and Now

The design of personal computers has changed dramatically since the introduction of the first home computers in the 1970s. You can read a brief history of the computer's development at these sites.

❯ **Choose two computers—one early design and one design from within the past five years—to compare.** With an adult's permission, use the internet and the library to research the design and development of each model. As you research, consider the following questions.

* What problem or need did the computer meet?

* What choices did the designers make during the design process to meet these needs?

* How is the computer's form related to its function?

* What aesthetic choices did the designers make? How did they reflect the tastes of the time?

* Did the designer consider ergonomics? Green design? If so, how?

* How did available technology influence the design?

* What design features are the same for both computers? Why?

* What changed in the design from the early computer to the recent computer? Why were those changes made?

❯ **Prepare a chart to compare and contrast** the two computer designs.

Try This!

Take a walk through your local electronics store or flip the pages of its latest catalog. Study the different computer models available and explore their design features, including screen size, color, shape, material, and technology. Which features are the same? Which are different? How do these features make the computer more attractive to a certain type of buyer?

Draw an Electrical Circuit Diagram

Electronics designers need to understand electricity, circuits, and circuit design. When drawing the design of a circuit, designers use symbols instead of words or pictures. A symbol is a sign, letter, or diagram that represents something. Circuit symbols make a diagram easy to understand. They are also universal, which means anyone who knows them can read the circuit diagram, no matter what language they speak. In circuit drawings, designers use many symbols. You can find a few important ones at this website.

🔎 dreamstime circuit symbols

An electrical circuit diagram shows the connections and components in a circuit. It does not show how they will be physically arranged on a circuit board, just how they are connected and how the electricity will flow. Creating a circuit diagram helps engineers better understand how to build a circuit.

For example, a simple circuit has four parts: a switch, a power source (battery), a load (light bulb), and a conductor (the wire). You can see other examples of simple circuit diagrams here.

🔎 beginners circuit diagram

❱ **Now it's your turn. Draw an electrical circuit diagram for each of the following scenarios.**

✱ Three D-cell batteries are placed in a battery pack to power a circuit containing three light bulbs.

✱ A single cell, light bulb, and switch are placed together in a circuit so that the switch can be opened and closed to turn the light bulb on.

✱ A three-pack of D-cell batteries is placed in a circuit to power a flashlight bulb.

Try This!

Design your own electrical circuit and draw a circuit diagram. Can other people understand it?

Think Like a Designer

Sometimes, industrial designers take a current product and make it better. They add or subtract features, change materials, or adjust the shape and size of an object to improve its design and make it more useful and attractive to consumers.

❯ **Make a list of the electronics you use every day,** such as smartphones, fitness watches, televisions, iPods, video game consoles, stereos, DVD players, calculators, alarm clocks, scales, and more. Choose one that you'd like to improve.

❯ **Think about the following questions.**

✱ What do you use this device for?

✱ What features does it have that you like? What features don't you like?

✱ What bothers you about the way it works?

✱ What features do you wish it had that it currently does not?

❯ **Think like a designer.** What changes would you make? What features would you add or subtract to improve the device's design? Make a design sketch to illustrate your ideas. Remember that designers draw several versions of a product before they choose a final design.

❯ **When you have chosen a final design, create a simple model.** How does your prototype feel when you hold it? Is it the right size? Can you use it comfortably? Do you need to make any changes to your design?

Try This!

Try to redesign a process instead of a product. Is there something you do every day, such as get dressed or walk to the bus stop, that you could change for the better?

COMPUTER-AIDED DESIGN

HOW'S THE TENT DESIGN COMING?

SO GOOD! THIS CAD PROGRAM IS TOTALLY AMAZING!

WHOAH! IS THAT A 3-D MODEL?

YEAH! AND CHECK THIS OUT...

IT CAN DO **ALL** KINDS OF SIMULATIONS.

THIS IS HOW OUR TENT WOULD HANDLE BEING IN A TORNADO.

CAN YOU EVEN IMAGINE HOW MUCH HARDER IT WAS TO DESIGN PRODUCTS BEFORE CAD?

IF WE WERE DOING THIS ON PAPER, WE WOULD HAVE NEEDED A TON OF ERASERS.

NOT TO MENTION ALL THE TIME WE'D HAVE SPENT LOOKING FOR TORNADOS TO TEST THE TENT!

Product design is more than creating something that looks good. Industrial designers need to understand how a product works to ensure that it also performs in a way that is helpful to the person using it.

With **computer-aided design (CAD)** software, designers can explore both the form and function of an idea for a design. CAD software allows pen-and-paper design to be done on a computer, making the design process faster and more efficient than ever before. Industrial designers in every production industry, from fashion to car manufacturing, use CAD software in the design process. No matter the product or the industry, CAD software allows designers to explore ideas, visualize designs, create **virtual** models, and produce them.

ESSENTIAL QUESTION

What benefits can beginner designers gain from using CAD? What are the drawbacks?

WORDS TO KNOW

computer-aided design (CAD): software used to create two-dimensional and three-dimensional drawings.

virtual: a computer version of something real.

drafting: drawing a plan of something to be constructed.

tedious: tiresome, slow, and dull.

computer-aided manufacturing (CAM): the use of computers to manufacture a part or prototype.

precision: accuracy.

HISTORY OF CAD

Before CAD software, all design work was done manually. For years, designers created new designs with pencils, paper, and other manual drawing and **drafting** tools. This meant the design process was extremely **tedious** and time-consuming! If they made a mistake, designers often had to start over.

During World War II, things began to slowly change. The war triggered the development of new technologies, mostly for military use, including the introduction of early computers. During the next few decades, technology improvements allowed computers to become smaller, faster, and more powerful. They also opened the door for the creation of CAD software.

The 1950s and 1960s saw the start of CAD software. In 1957, Patrick Hanratty (1942–), developed the first commercial **computer-aided manufacturing (CAM)** system while working at General Electric. His system, named PRONTO (Program for Numerical Tooling Operations), was used to automate machine tools in the manufacturing process.

Designing with CAD

credit: Thomas-Soellner

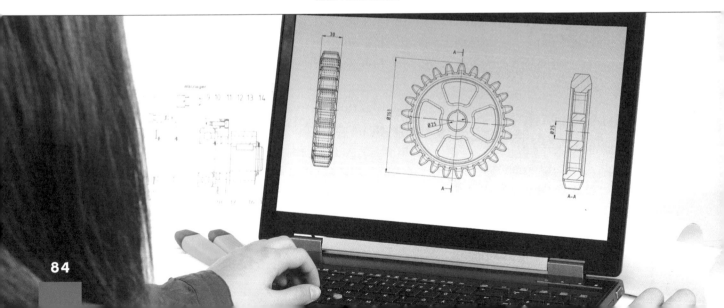

Five years later in 1963, Ivan Sutherland (1938–) developed Sketchpad, an innovative CAD software program, while working at the Massachusetts Institute of Technology. When using Sketchpad, a designer interacted with the computer by using a light pen to draw on the computer monitor. The work of these two men—Hanratty and Sutherland—set the stage for the CAD software of today. Their early versions of CAD software formed the basis for more complex software programs in the future.

The aerospace and automotive industries were some of the first users of CAD software.

These industries wanted to take advantage of CAD's greater **precision** and speed as compared to traditional manual design techniques. At the time, you couldn't buy a CAD software program at the store. Instead, companies had their own programmers develop custom CAD programs that were specific to their products and needs. Hanratty helped to design one of these CAD systems, named DAC (Design Automated by Computer), at General Motors Research Laboratories in the mid-1960s.

DID YOU KNOW?

Sutherland's Sketchpad required so much computer power it could be run only on the MIT Lincoln Labs' TX-2 computer—one of the world's largest computers at the time.

Beyond Product Design

CAD software can be useful in areas other than product design. For example, some CAD software allows designers to create specific tools to manufacture a certain product. Other CAD software might let designers find the most efficient layout for a factory. And some software helps determine what to do with a product when it reaches the end of its usable life.

In the 1970s, the first 3-D CAD software was developed. For the first time, designers could create and view a 3-D image of their design on a screen. General CAD software also hit the market, allowing more people and industries to adopt CAD as part of the product-design process. In 1981, International Business Machines (IBM) introduced the first personal computer. This technology milestone marked the beginning of an extensive adoption of CAD software for design. Today, CAD is used in a wide range of industries for a variety of design projects.

HOW DESIGNERS USE CAD

CAD software can perform many complex tasks. Product designers use CAD programs to design a product and document the design process. For many designers, CAD software has replaced traditional pen-and-paper drawings with computer-generated sketches. With CAD, designers can create either 2-D drawings or 3-D models that can be rotated and viewed from any angle. They look almost exactly like the finished product.

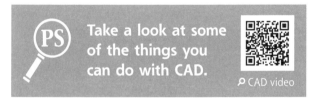

PS Take a look at some of the things you can do with CAD.

🔍 CAD video

Two-dimensional CAD models are flat, 2-D drawings. They show an object's overall **dimensions**—how tall, long, and wide it is. They illustrate its layout and provide information needed to build the object. Three-dimensional CAD models show more detail about each individual component of the product. In addition to showing an object's size and shape, 3-D CAD models show how these components fit and work together. For manufacturers that produce products with many intricate parts, a 3-D CAD model can be very helpful.

Using CAD speeds up the production process. When designers need to make a change, they no longer have to redraw entire designs or blueprints. Instead, they can use the CAD digital file and make only the necessary changes, while keeping the rest of the design the same. When the design is finished, CAD software produces electronic files for manufacturing or machining. This output also has information about materials, processes, dimensions, and more.

DID YOU KNOW?

Almost no product today is created without the use of CAD software.

CAD does a lot more than simply let designers draw sketches and build virtual models.

Today's CAD software allows designers to fully analyze their designs through **simulations**. A simulation creates a virtual environment that looks, feels, and behaves like the real world to test the design. Without creating a physical prototype, designers can use a simulation to test their model to see how it reacts to heat, pressure, physical forces, and other conditions. In simulations, designers can figure out the strengths and weaknesses of their design without having to build a physical model. This saves a lot of time and money.

WORDS TO KNOW

computer-aided industrial design (CAID): a type of design software used to create the look and feel of products, often with increased creativity than traditional design software.

technical: relating to scientific or mechanical methods.

texture mapping: the application of patterns or images to the surface of a 3-D model to make it look more realistic.

vector image: a digital image that is saved in the computer's memory as points, lines, and shapes.

prosthetic: an artificial body part.

For example, a simulation of a chair design might explore how the chair reacts to different amounts of weight. If the virtual chair model cracks under a certain weight, designers can go back to the original design and adjust it to make the chair sturdier and better able to handle greater weights.

In addition, CAD software can simulate how a design would work in extreme environments that would be hard to create and test in the real world, such as a tent in a tornado. CAD software allows designers and engineers to discover flaws and fix them before production begins, saving money and time.

DID YOU KNOW?

While most professional product designers use commercial CAD software, several free programs exist for beginners to work with and gain experience. To learn more, visit this website.

🔎 top free CAD

COMPUTER-AIDED INDUSTRIAL DESIGN

Computer-aided industrial design (CAID) is a type of CAD software. Both CAID and CAD software enable a designer to create a 3-D model of a product before manufacturing begins. However, CAID software is generally more artistic, while CAD is more **technical**.

CAID software gives designers more freedom to easily experiment with an object's shape and form. With CAID software, industrial designers can use many visualization tools. They can create images that look as real as a photograph. They can apply patterns or images to a 3-D model to make the surface appear more realistic, a process called **texture mapping**. The designer can also highlight different surfaces on a model, making it appear as realistic as possible.

While the design process in CAID is more artistic, it is also less precise than CAD. Often, designers will use both types of software. They might create a new design in CAID, then prepare design files that can work in a CAD system. In CAD, the design team can focus on the more technical aspects of the design, testing and preparing it for physical production.

PRECISION AND CONTROL

Using CAD for product design has many advantages. One of the biggest advantages is that it gives designers more precision and control when creating digital sketches and 3-D models. Even the most precise sketches or pencil drawings will have some small errors, however. In comparison, when creating a drawing or model, CAD software uses **vector images**. Vector images use mathematical equations to draw a design. The software translates the mathematical equations into points connected with lines or curves. These make up all the different shapes you see in the CAD graphic. Vector images allow designers to change the scale of the design without sacrificing accuracy.

Making a Prosthetic Limb

One day, CAD could be used to make **prosthetic** limbs. Traditionally, prosthetics are made by hand through casting and producing a mold from which the prosthetic is formed. With CAD, designers could use a scanner to get a digital image of the patient's limb and socket. Then, they could turn that scanned image into a 3-D model with CAD software. They could adjust the model as needed and send the digital files to a manufacturer to make the limb. One 2017 study compared the two methods of making prosthetic legs for patients who'd had their lower leg amputated between the ankle and knee. The patients who received a prosthetic leg made with CAD technology reported adapting much more quickly to their new limb than those who received one made from traditional methods. The CAD group walked farther and reported less pain.

Designers also use tools in CAD to draw more accurately. One of these tools is **grid snapping**, which uses an invisible grid to place lines on perfect horizontal and vertical lines. This way, designers can more easily ensure their design is a specific length, area, or volume.

SEEING A DESIGN IN 3-D

In industrial design, being able to see a product in three dimensions is critical. It's the best way to see if a design works the way it is meant to and if it is aesthetically pleasing. Traditional paper sketches were unable to do this—it's hard to make a 3-D object on a 2-D piece of paper. Using CAD software makes it possible for designers to easily create 3-D designs. They can design in three dimensions from the very beginning or extend 2-D designs into three dimensions.

3-D Printing

Three-dimensional printing is one of the most exciting applications of CAD designs. A 3-D printer lays down layer after layer of a material to build almost any kind of physical object from a 3-D digital model. Objects of almost any shape

credit: enmyo

can be produced. Designers have used 3-D printers to create physical prototypes and models. For example, these printers are being used in the automotive and aerospace industries, and even in healthcare.

Designing in 3-D has several advantages. First, it gives designers the ability to create a virtual object that looks like the finished product. With CAD software, designers can view the virtual model from all angles and even move around the model. Designers can also look at the internal parts of a virtual object by making the outer layers transparent. Being able to see a virtual finished product makes it easier for designers to find and fix any flaws. It's also a great way to show customers a product and get their input and any suggested changes before production begins.

DID YOU KNOW? One of the best-known CAD programs in product design is SolidWorks, a solid modeling software that allows designers to create and edit 3-D solids quickly and efficiently. Do you ever use a CamelBak when you hike or ride your bike? There's a good chance it was designed using SolidWorks!

Before CAD software, many of these changes happened during the prototype stage of the design process. CAD reduces the need for multiple physical prototypes at every step of the design process, which lowers costs and shortens the time needed to finish a design.

With CAD software's 3-D virtual objects, product designers work more efficiently, saving time and money.

Before CAD, if designers wanted to create a new version of an existing product, they would have to create a brand-new sketch by hand. If they made any errors in the new sketch, they'd have to grab an eraser or start all over. It could take a lot of time!

With CAD, these problems are solved. If designers make an error, they can often remove it by simply clicking "Undo." Larger edits are just as simple. Each individual piece of a design can be edited, without changing other objects or lines in the overall design. Designers can also fix a big problem by simply opening an earlier version of the design file and going back to a point before the error occurred.

WORDS TO KNOW

code: another name for a computer program.

hinder: to hold back or create difficulties for.

conversion software: software that changes paper sketches into a vector image.

When creating a new version of an existing product, CAD makes the process much simpler. Designers no longer have to start from the very beginning of the design process. Instead, they can open an existing design file and edit the features they want to change. With a few clicks, they can change colors and materials. This makes it quicker and easier to create a custom design!

Designs created in CAD software can be tested to see how they respond to a variety of situations and environments.

In many cases, the CAD virtual design can replace a physical prototype in the design process. Designs created in CAD software can also be converted directly into **code** for various computer-controlled manufacturing machines. This can make the production process more accurate and efficient.

Engineers design and print a part for an aluminum aircraft
credit: Kelly White, U.S. Air Force

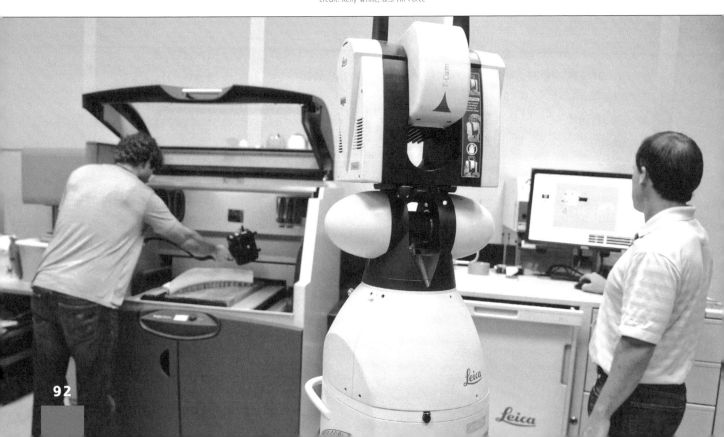

DRAWBACKS TO CAD SOFTWARE

While CAD software has many benefits, it's not always the perfect solution. Some people believe the traditional method of sketching with pencil and paper helps designers find a solution to the original design problem more quickly. Sketching can help develop a designer's ability to find innovative solutions. Replacing traditional sketching with a computer screen and a mouse might **hinder** the creative process.

In addition, designing in CAD could cause designers to focus too much on how a product looks instead of what it is supposed to do. Computers can make designers more efficient and effective, but if the design team focuses too much on technology and doesn't spend enough time understanding the problem, the slick-looking product it creates might not meet people's needs.

DID YOU KNOW?

CAD software is used to create computer animation for special effects in movies and advertising.

To address these drawbacks, some CAD software programs have added virtual sketching tools. With a graphics tablet and other touch screens, designers can "sketch" their designs by hand on a virtual surface. The sketch is then converted into a digital file. This approach is helping re-ignite the creative spark in design problem solving while using CAD software. Designers who prefer paper-and-pencil sketches can use **conversion software**, which takes their paper sketches and turns them into usable vector images in CAD.

CAD software can be used to design virtually anything, from a coffee cup to a race car. When you look around your house, just about everything you see, including your toaster, couch, and gaming console, was probably once a 3-D virtual model designed with CAD software. While this tool can help designers be more effective and efficient, it doesn't change the overall goal of industrial design—to solve a problem.

ESSENTIAL QUESTION

What benefits can beginner designers gain from using CAD? What are the drawbacks?

CAD Design: Learn the Basics

You can learn the basics of CAD using Tinkercad, a simple, online 3-D design and printing app. Many people, including designers, hobby enthusiasts, and crafters, use Tinkercad to make prototypes, toys, jewelry, and more. If you want to learn how to make your own CAD designs, you'll first have to learn the basics—how to operate the controls, how to change views, add shapes, resize figures, and more.

Here's a short video about Tinkercad.

❯ **Get started at the Tinkercad website.** You'll need an adult's permission to create a free account on the site.

❯ **Once you have an account, you can move on to the "6 Basic Skills" lessons.** Complete each one.

❯ **After you finish these lessons, create a new project.** Use this file to practice the skills that you just learned until you feel comfortable manipulating objects and work planes. Practice all of the skills, including the following.

* Add objects to the work plane
* Group objects
* Ungroup objects
* Change size
* Move location
* Cut out material
* Change color
* Add numbers/letters

❯ **Explore the design desktop.** Can you find the following features? Experiment using these features in a simple design.

* Characters
* Shape generator
* Flip

Try This!

Tinkercad has two features that allow you to change your design into blocks or bricks. Where are these features on the desktop? Explore how they work.

Create a Scale Model with CAD

Designers can use CAD software to make a scale model of a product. A scale model is a copy of an object that is usually smaller than the actual size of the object. Designers use a scale model to see how an object will look in real life. A scale model can also be used as a guide when building a full-size object.

▶ **First, select a famous landmark,** such as the Eiffel Tower, the Empire State Building, the Washington Monument, or Big Ben. Head to the library or, with an adult's permission, use the internet to research the landmark and find its dimensions, its main construction materials, and other important facts about the landmark.

▶ **Use Tinkercad to make a model of the landmark.** You'll have to convert the landmark's dimensions using a scale factor. For example, 1 centimeter = 10 meters. If the landmark is 500 meters tall and 100 meters wide at its base in the real world, you would convert it to 50 centimeters tall (500m ÷ 10) and 10 centimeters wide (100m ÷ 10) for the model. This keeps the proportion of the landmark's height and width the same for the real landmark and the model.

▶ **After you complete your model, have someone review it and give feedback.** Based on their comments, redesign and adjust the model. Repeat this process until no more revisions are needed.

DID YOU KNOW?

Have you ever done a Lego kit and followed the instructions to build a specific design? In 2012, the Lego company used CAD to design a 8.5-foot-tall dinosaur model!

Try This!

Make a model of the same landmark, only make it twice the size. How can you easily accomplish this?

Create Your Own Design in CAD

❯ **Using Tinkercad, create your own design of an object from scratch.** Some ideas include a keychain, pencil holder, toy boat, or stencil. Make sure to follow the design process.

* Understand the problem
* Develop a solution
* Define the design requirements
* Create a model/prototype
* Generate product ideas and solutions
* Test and redesign
* Select the best idea

❯ **After you have the final design, consider the following questions.**

* How did using Tinkercad make the design process faster and easier?
* Did you find any drawbacks to using CAD software?

Try This!

If you have access to a 3-D printer, get permission to print your design. Did it turn out the way you expected? Explain.

Shanghai Tower

Shanghai Tower in China has the world's fastest elevators and the world's highest observation desk in a building, and is the second-tallest building in the world. It was designed using CAD. The software helped engineers and designers plan for the extremely windy conditions of Shanghai. The team could test the building design against strong wind without having to build it first!

CHANGING NEEDS,
CHANGING SOLUTIONS

Every product begins with a design. Whether it's a chair, cell phone, or coffeemaker, all the products we use got their start from a design. Industrial designers consider both form and function to provide the best user experience and even spark an emotional connection with users. How well they do this often determines a product's success.

Good industrial design is more important than ever in today's connected, global marketplace. To produce their best designs, industrial designers must understand their customers' changing needs. At the same time, they need to incorporate new trends into their designs. In the coming years, designers will need to consider a variety of factors, from **sustainable** solutions to the **Internet of Things (IoT)** in their design solutions.

ESSENTIAL QUESTION

What might the future of industrial design look like?

WORDS TO KNOW

sustainable: designed to minimize environmental impact.

Internet of Things (IoT): everyday devices that are connected to the internet and have tiny sensors that gather, store, and process data.

sustainability: meeting the needs of the present without harming the ability of future generations to meet their needs.

life cycle: the stages of a product's life, from manufacture to disposal.

disposal: the process of throwing away or getting rid of something.

toxin: a poisonous or harmful substance.

SUSTAINABLE SOLUTIONS

Around the world, **sustainability** is a hot topic, even though many people do not know exactly what it means. For some people, the concept of sustainability means protecting the environment. However, sustainability involves much more than being environmentally friendly.

According to the United Nations, sustainable design or development is "development that meets the needs of the present without compromising the ability of future generations to meet their own needs." This involves balancing the needs of the environment along with the needs of the world's people and economies.

This building was designed with space for growing trees. How is this an example of sustainable design? How do the trees and plants contribute to the health of people who live and work in this building?

Designers are increasingly being asked to come up with sustainable solutions in their product designs. One way designers are doing this is by designing for a product's entire **life cycle**. Many steps are involved to get a product to your house. From manufacturing and transport to use and **disposal**, each step is part of the product's life cycle. At each step, there are opportunities to reduce energy use or minimize waste.

For products to be sustainable, designers make choices to use fewer materials, reduce energy use, and reduce waste.

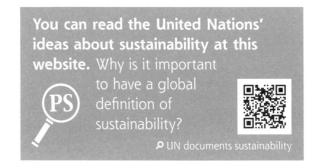

You can read the United Nations' ideas about sustainability at this website. Why is it important to have a global definition of sustainability?

🔎 UN documents sustainability

Green Materials

Sustainable design includes choosing green materials with the following characteristics.

› **Nontoxic:** Do not leak **toxins** into the environment as they decompose.

› **Abundant:** Raw materials that exist in large quantities and are not at risk of being depleted.

› **Easily reproduced:** Can be easily grown, harvested, and regrown.

› **Rapidly renewable:** Quick to reproduce, such as bamboo, organic cotton, cork, and natural rubber.

› **Low waste:** Produce little waste during production.

› **Recycled, recyclable, or biodegradable:** Have already been used, can be used as another product, or safely decompose back into the earth. Such materials create less waste and save energy that otherwise would be needed to prepare new materials for use.

WORDS TO KNOW

recycled: converted into usable material.

finite: having a limit.

greenhouse gas: a gas in the atmosphere that traps heat and has been linked to global warming.

global warming: a gradual increase in the overall temperature of the earth's atmosphere.

carbon footprint: the total amount of carbon dioxide and other greenhouse gases emitted over the full life cycle of a product or service, or by a person, family, or community in a year.

light weighting: creating designs that use few materials.

They choose green materials that are nontoxic to the environment. They create designs that minimize a product's energy use. They search for ways to reduce waste during manufacturing. They also try to create products that can be **recycled** or reused at the end of the life cycle, instead of being thrown away. With sustainable design, industrial designers can make responsible choices about their product designs.

ENERGY-EFFICIENT DESIGN

Around the world, people are becoming more aware of the importance of conserving energy. Traditional fossil fuel energy sources such as coal and oil are **finite** and reserves are running low. In addition, these fuel sources can harm the environment.

Design for Social Impact

If you ever listen to or watch the news, you'll know that there are people around the world who need help. Whether someone is a refugee fleeing a civil war or a person with a disability, their lives can be improved through industrial design. A lightweight backpack, a portable solar light, a secure pill bottle that can be easily opened—these are all examples of designs that help improve lives. What challenges do you see in your daily life that could be solved with a better design?

Burning fossil fuels releases carbon dioxide and other **greenhouse gases** into the atmosphere, which have been linked to **global warming**. As a result, manufacturers are increasingly concerned with the amount of energy they use during production. Consumers are becoming more and more aware of how much energy they use every day and the size of the **carbon footprint** they are leaving on the planet.

With this heightened awareness of energy use, the need for energy-efficient solutions has become more important than ever.

Today, you can buy energy-efficient lighting, windows, dishwashers, freezers, refrigerators, and doors. And that's not all! These products and many others will become even more common in the coming years as designers create increasingly energy-efficient products.

DID YOU KNOW?

Light weighting is a sustainable design strategy that focuses on making a product with fewer materials, making it lighter in both weight and environmental impact.

USER EXPERIENCE DESIGN

In recent years, user experience (UX) design has been an important part of good product design. UX design results in products that are both usable and give consumers pleasure. It focuses on every part of a person's experience with a product.

For example, a smartphone might look good, but if it is difficult to set up and does not integrate well with other technology that you use, it probably won't be the best experience. Will you tell your friends to buy it?

WORDS TO KNOW

sensor: a device that measures and records physical properties.

embed: to put something firmly inside of something else.

How is user experience formed? When you get a new smartphone, you form a quick impression of it—maybe you like it or maybe you don't. As time passes and you use the phone, your impression of it evolves. During this time, you form a memorable user experience—either good or bad.

When designers understand how user experience is formed, they can use this information to create a better design. To do this, designers consider a product's why, what, and how. Why do users select a product? What do they want to do with it? How can the design meet functional needs in an easy-to-use and pleasing way? By addressing each of these questions, designers can create better products that provide meaningful experiences for users.

One great example of successful UX design is Apple's iPhone.

When it first came out, the iPhone delivered a user experience that was miles ahead of any other cell phone of its time. Other companies saw Apple's success with a product that delivered a great user experience and they joined in, too.

Product designers work closely with product managers during the design process. They constantly test new ideas and prototypes with customers. For example, GoPro is a successful company that makes action cameras. GoPro incorporates UX design in all its products to provide the best user experience for its customers. It only manufactures a product after it has been completely approved through customer feedback.

Check out these videos from GoPro users! How does the design of these cameras help users be creative and innovative? 🔎 16 must-see GoPro

To understand user experience firsthand, the company has a program that gives their employees time off to explore their interests and record their experiences using a GoPro camera. The program turns employees into users and helps the company better understand and improve the user experience.

SMART AND CONNECTED

Smart products are everywhere. Smart refrigerators, electrical sockets, home security systems, and motion **sensors** are just a few of the smart products that you might have in your home. Smart products incorporate good design and the latest technology. Designing these products takes the effort of an entire team of experts, from industrial designers to software engineers.

Many of these smart products are also connected to the internet. They are part of a group of devices called the Internet of Things (IoT). The IoT is a group of everyday objects that are connected to the internet and to each other. They are **embedded** with tiny sensors and software that manage the device's operation and collect and exchange data through the internet.

WORDS TO KNOW

globalization: the integration of the world economy through trade, money, and labor.

interconnected: being related to one another.

interdependent: two or more people or things that are dependent on each other.

server: a computer that processes requests and provides data to other computers over a network connection.

network: a group of computers and related devices such as printers that are connected to each other.

cloud-based: computing applications, services, or resources that are available on demand via the internet and are housed by a cloud-computing provider.

Devices that are part of the IoT aren't the normal computers and laptops that you use to surf the web. Instead, these devices are ones that traditionally were not connected to the internet or can communicate with the internet without human action. That's why a smartphone is not considered an IoT device, but a fitness band is. Some experts predict that more than 20 billion IoT devices will be in use by 2020.

For designers, the data gathered by IoT devices can be extremely useful. Before, some design flaws could only be discovered after a product was launched to the public and a lot of people were using it. Companies gathered feedback about their products through meetings and discussions with customers—which can be very time consuming.

IoT devices, however, can gather data about operations and send it to company engineers and designers automatically.

Global Design

Through **globalization**, the world is becoming more **interconnected** and **interdependent**. Money, technology, raw materials, and finished goods move quickly across borders. Because of globalization, companies can sell products all across the world. Industrial designers must therefore consider the different cultures, beliefs, tastes, and preferences of a global customer. Many global companies, such as Nike, have found success building a core product with different versions that are a good fit for specific global areas and customers.

The company learns how customers are using the product and which features are the most popular and which are barely touched. The company can also learn which parts of the product are not working as designed. All this information helps designers adjust and improve their designs.

CAD IN THE CLOUD

Traditional product design has taken place step-by-step. Each step is finished before the next one begins. But in some companies, teams are working on different steps and tasks at the same time. Often, team members are in different physical locations—one may work at home in Boston, another at company headquarters in Chicago, and a third at a contractor's office in Spain.

While CAD software has made the design process more efficient in many ways, it continues to change to adapt to the new ways people are working together. Some companies are turning to **cloud-based** software to allow multiple people to work on different parts of a design project at the same time, from anywhere in the world. With cloud-based computing, team members can use CAD software at any time, from any location if they have an internet connection.

As teams work together on the project, any changes to the design are communicated to each member almost instantaneously. As a result, innovation can soar and any design issues can be identified and fixed early.

What Is Cloud Computing?

Cloud computing is the delivery of computing services, such as **servers**, storage, databases, **networks**, software, and more, through the internet. Simply put, instead of keeping computer hardware and software on a server in its office, a company hires a cloud provider to handle information for it offsite. The provider maintains the necessary server and storage hardware that process and store the company's information. When the company needs its information or needs to use an application, employees can simply access it via the internet.

VIRTUAL AND AUGMENTED REALITY

CAD software allows designers to view their designs in 3-D. New **virtual reality (VR)** and **augmented reality (AR)** design tools take this one step further, giving designers an even more realistic view of how their design will look.

VR is computer simulation that allows users to interact in a realistic way within an environment. Users see a 3-D display through a headset. By moving their head, they see up, down, and side to side. In product design, VR enables designers to better see and interact with a virtual model through every stage of the design and manufacturing process. They can find and fix problems before a physical prototype is made or production begins.

With advanced computer technology, VR prototypes can look and feel exactly as the product will in real life.

VR also creates an **immersive** experience for a customer. By putting on a VR headset, customers can interact and experience a product in an almost lifelike way. Then, they can suggest improvements or changes they would like to see or point out any problems they discover in the product's ergonomics.

If you have a VR headset, you can take an immersive journey through the national parks!

PS

𝒫 VR national parks

Augmented reality technology is like VR, but unlike VR, it allows users to maintain full awareness of the real world. AR **superimposes** additional information onto users' views of their surroundings. This provides users with additional data, but still allows them to interact with the actual environment.

Some users have likened AR technology to having X-ray vision. AR technology can be used to simulate a product and how it works in the real world before it is even built.

Designers can also use AR to check the ergonomics of a product. For example, they could test an AR version of a new gaming controller to see if the controls are in the right position or if they should be moved. Design and production engineers can redesign and retest with virtual prototypes until they get the design just right.

Industrial design has come a long way since craftspeople designed and created individual goods. Today, designers use sophisticated technology and software to help them create products that people want and need and enjoy using. Still, the goal is the same—finding a way to solve a problem.

ESSENTIAL QUESTION

What might the future of industrial design look like?

Design an Ergonomic Remote Control

Designers consider ergonomics in each product they create. Ergonomics is the process of designing products or arranging workplaces that are safe, comfortable, and easy to use.

An important part of ergonomics is **anthropometry**, which is the measurement of the human body. People come in many shapes and sizes. Designers and engineers use human body measurements such as height or arm length when they design products. In this activity, you'll be a designer creating an ergonomic remote control for a friend.

❯ **First, review the remote control's design requirements.** The remote will be used to turn a television on and off, change channels, raise or lower the volume, and play DVDs. The remote must include the following buttons: power, play, numbers 0 through 9, stop, volume up and down, pause, channel up and down, fast forward, mute, and rewind.

❯ **Next, observe how your friend uses a remote control.** Have them hold one in their hand and ask them to do the following:

* Press the on/off button

* Press the numbers 0–9 buttons

* Press the channel up and down buttons

❯ **For each movement, what finger(s) did he or she use to press the button?** How did he or she hold the remote when pressing the button? What position was it in? Was it easy or hard to reach the button? Record your observations in your design notebook.

❯ **Based on your observations of how your friend used the remote** and the design requirements, choose 10 parts of your friend's hand to measure. Use these measurements to choose the right length, width, and height for the remote and where to place the buttons on the remote.

WORDS TO KNOW

anthropometry: the scientific study of the measurements and proportions of the human body.

❯ **Next, create a sketch of your remote control design.** Include measurements in your sketch. You may find it helpful to create a series of sketches, with each incorporating more detail. When you have finished the sketches, build a prototype of your remote design using cardboard, cardstock, or another material. Does your prototype's measurements match your design sketch? If it is too long or too wide, make adjustments as needed.

❯ **When the prototype is complete, have your friend hold it and press the buttons.** Are they able to use the remote easily and comfortably? Are there any changes that you could make to the design to make it more comfortable and easy-to-use? Make these changes and re-test the prototype with your friend.

❯ **Were the hand measurements you made in this activity useful** when designing the remote control? Explain. Were there any hand measurements would you use in future remote designs that you did not use? Why?

DID YOU KNOW?

The word "ergonomics" comes from two Greek words: *ergo* meaning "work" and *nomos* meaning "laws."

Consider This!

What other devices do you use that could be improved to make them easier and more comfortable to use? What measurements would you have to take to create a more ergonomic design?

What's Your Carbon Footprint?

Now and in the future, designers are being asked to create sustainable product designs. One measure of a sustainable design is how much it adds to your carbon footprint. Your carbon footprint is a measure of how much carbon dioxide you emit as a result of your daily activities. By understanding what goes into your carbon footprint, you can become a better designer for sustainable solutions.

To know your carbon footprint, you'll look at four main sources of carbon dioxide in your life: housing and home energy use, transportation, daily habits, and recycling. Assign each category a color. You'll create a drawing to represent your carbon footprint by adding rings of color around a central core. The more rings you have, the larger your carbon footprint.

❯ **To estimate your footprint, answer the following questions.**

1. Housing and Home Energy Use

✱ Do you live in a single-family home (4 rings) or an apartment or multi-family dwelling (2 rings)

✱ Do you use energy-efficient light bulbs? Yes (0 rings) or no (1 ring)

✱ Do you have a programmable thermostat? Yes (0 rings) or no (1 ring)

✱ Do you use Energy Star appliances? Yes (0 rings) or no (1 ring)

2. Transportation

✱ Does your family own a car(s)? For each small car (1 ring), medium, or large car (2 rings)

✱ Do you regularly change the air filter on your car and check the tire pressure? Yes (0 rings) or no (1 ring)

✱ Have you flown on an airplane in the past year? Yes (1 ring) or no (0 rings)

3. Daily Habits

* Are you a vegetarian? Yes (1 ring) or no (2 rings)

* Do you eat organic food? Yes (0 rings) or no (1 ring)

* Do you take baths or run the water when brushing your teeth or washing dishes? Yes (1 ring) or no (0 rings)

* Do you water your grass several times a week? Yes (1 ring) or no (0 rings)

4. Recycling

* Do you recycle household trash? Yes (1 ring) or no (2 rings)

* Do you compose kitchen and yard waste? Yes (0 rings) or no (1 ring)

> **Look at your drawing—how big is your carbon footprint?**

* Which sources contribute the most to your carbon footprint?

* What can you and your family do to reduce the size of your carbon footprint?

* How could design help you reduce your carbon footprint?

Consider This!

Greenhouse gases trap more heat in the earth's atmosphere, raising temperatures. The warmer temperatures are causing changes around the world on land, in the oceans, and in the air, which could greatly affect life on Earth. How does this motivate you to reduce your carbon footprint?

Design a Green Can Holder

When you buy a six-pack of soda at the store, a plastic connector holds the cans together. While this design works well for its purpose, it is not environmentally friendly. When the plastic connectors are thrown in the trash, wild animals can get tangled in them. Plus, plastic can take hundreds of years to decompose and may leak pollutants into the environment. Can you come up with a green design for a can holder that solves these problems?

Your task is to design a holder for six cans that is environmentally friendly, animal safe, easy to use, and convenient. Gather the following materials to use in your product.

* 6 soda cans
* cardboard
* paper

* duct tape
* wax paper
* string

* scissors
* paint stirrers
* rubber bands

> **Brainstorm some potential ideas.** As you brainstorm, think about the following questions.

* What other types of containers/ holders already exist for cans?
* How will you hold the cans together?

* How will you carry the holder?
* How will you remove cans from the holder?

> **Sketch a few of your ideas.** Do you need any other materials?

Using your materials, build a prototype of your can holder. Once complete, test it. Does it work? Does it bend or twist? How can you make it sturdier? What are its weaknesses? How does the holder help the environment?

Consider This!

What would happen to your holder at disposal? Are the materials that you used recyclable? If not, could you redesign the holder using all recyclable materials?

Improving Existing Design

Industrial designers find ways to improve existing designs. Sometimes, designers take existing products and make them more sustainable and environmentally friendly by changing the amount and type of materials used in the product or changing the product's packaging.

❯ **Search your house for several examples of products that could be more sustainable or environmentally friendly.** Use the design process to develop a solution to improve the original design.

❯ **Share your proposed design solution with your classmates.**

Consider This!

Did the changes you make to improve the product's sustainability also affect any other aspect of the product? Are these effects positive or negative? Explain.

Candles Forever!

You might not think you could improve on the design of a candle. After all, for centuries, people have relied on the same basic candle design. But you can improve on the candle holder! Designer Benjamin Shine created a candle holder that catches the melted wax and shapes it into a brand-new candle as the first candle burns. Two candles for the price of one!

3-D printer: a printer that creates three-dimensional objects—that have length, width, and height—using a range of materials.

accelerate: to increase the speed of an object over time.

accessory: something added to something else to make it more useful or add features.

advantage: something helpful.

aesthetics: a set of principles concerned with nature and the appreciation of beauty.

alabaster: a soft mineral or rock that is often carved.

alloy: a substance made of two or more metals or of a metal and a nonmetal that are united (usually by melting them together).

anthropometry: the scientific study of the measurements and proportions of the human body.

architect: a person who designs buildings.

artifact: an object made by people in the past, including tools, pottery, and jewelry.

atom: a very small piece of matter. Atoms are the tiny building blocks of everything in the universe.

audio: relating to sound.

augmented reality (AR): a technology that superimposes a computer-generated image on a user's view of the real world.

ball bearing: a part of a wheel that uses small metal balls to reduce friction between the wheel and a fixed axle.

ballcock: a valve that automatically fills a tank after liquid has been drawn from it.

blacksmith: a person who makes things out of iron.

brainstorm: to think creatively and without judgment, often in a group of people.

brand identity: the message the consumer receives from a product, person, or thing.

brittleness: easily damaged or broken.

byproduct: a secondary product made in the manufacture of something else.

carbon footprint: the total amount of carbon dioxide and other greenhouse gases emitted over the full life cycle of a product or service, or by a person, family, or community in a year.

carbonized: coated with carbon.

chamber pot: a bowl-shaped pot used as an indoor toilet.

charge: a force of electricity that can be either positive or negative.

circuit: a path for electric current to flow, beginning and ending at the same point.

cistern: a tank for storing water.

civilization: a community of people that is advanced in art, science, and government.

cloud-based: computing applications, services, or resources that are available on demand via the internet and are housed by a cloud-computing provider.

code: another name for a computer program.

commission: an instruction given to another person, such as an artist, for a piece of work.

component: a part of a larger whole, especially a part of a machine.

computer-aided design (CAD): software used to create two-dimensional and three-dimensional drawings.

computer-aided industrial design (CAID): a type of design software used to create the look and feel of products, often with increased creativity than traditional design software.

computer-aided manufacturing (CAM): the use of computers to manufacture a part or prototype.

conductor: a material through which electricity moves easily.

conservation: preventing the overuse of a resource.

console: a specialized computer used to play video games on a TV screen.

consumer: a person who buys goods and services.

contaminate: to pollute or make dirty.

conversion software: software that changes paper sketches into a vector image.

criteria: the standard by which something is judged or measured.

data: information, often given in the form of numbers, that can be processed by a computer.

decision matrix: a table used to evaluate possible alternatives.

designer: someone who plans the form, look, and workings of a product based on the experiences of the user.

design requirements: the important characteristics that a solution must have to be successful.

device: a piece of equipment, such as a phone or MP3 player, that is made for a specific purpose.

differentiate: to make different through development or design.

digital: data expressed in a series of the digits 0 and 1.

dimension: a measurement such as height, length, width, and depth.

disc jockey: someone who plays recorded music at an event or on the radio.

disposal: the process of throwing away or getting rid of something.

diversify: becoming more varied.

domestic: related to the running of a home or family.

drafting: drawing a plan of something to be constructed.

durable: able to last.

DVD: a disc that can store large amounts of data.

economy: the way goods and services are bought and sold in a society.

electron: a particle in an atom with a negative charge.

embed: to put something firmly inside of something else.

energy efficient: using less energy to provide the same results.

engineer: a person who uses science, math, and creativity to design and build things.

ergonomics: the study of people and their working conditions.

exterior: the outside surface.

feasible: possible to do easily or conveniently.

filament: a very fine wire or thread.

finite: having a limit.

flammable: easily set on fire.

flash memory: a type of memory chip that is used to store and transfer data between a computer and digital devices.

format: the way data is organized.

form: how something looks.

fossil fuel: a natural fuel, such as coal, oil, or gas, formed during many years from the remains of living things.

freehand: drawn manually without the help of instruments such as rulers.

friction: the resistance that one surface or object encounters when moving over another.

function: how something works. To work or operate in a particular, correct way.

garderobe: a small chamber with a platform over a hole in the floor, used as a toilet.

GLOSSARY

gigabyte (GB): a unit of information equal to 1 billion.

globalization: the integration of the world economy through trade, money, and labor.

global warming: a gradual increase in the overall temperature of the earth's atmosphere.

green design: an approach to design that minimizes harmful effects on human health and the environment.

greenhouse gas: a gas in the atmosphere that traps heat and has been linked to global warming.

grid snapping: in software, the use of an invisible grid to place lines on perfect horizontal and vertical lines.

hard drive: a storage device for data.

hardware: the physical parts of an electronic device, such as the case, keyboard, screen, and speakers.

hinder: to hold back or create difficulties for.

iconic: a widely recognized symbol of a certain time.

ideation: the creative process of generating and developing ideas.

immersive: a 3-D image that appears to surround the user.

industrial design: the process of designing goods for mass production.

Industrial Revolution: a period of time in the eighteenth and nineteenth centuries when large-scale production of goods began.

integrate: to become part of.

interaction: how things work together.

interchangeable: two things that can be used in place of each other.

interconnected: being related to one another.

interdependent: two or more people or things that are dependent on each other.

Internet of Things (IoT): everyday devices that are connected to the internet and have tiny sensors that gather, store, and process data.

kinescope: a process that uses a special motion picture camera to photograph a television monitor.

layout: the way the parts of something are arranged.

licensed: granted permission to do something.

life cycle: the stages of a product's life, from manufacture to disposal.

light weighting: creating designs that use few materials.

logo: a symbol used to identify a company that appears on its products and in its marketing.

loop: a process that, upon reaching the end, returns to the beginning to start over.

magnetic tape: a medium for magnetic recording, made of a thin, magnetizable coating on a long, narrow strip of plastic film.

maneuver: movements made with skill and care.

manipulate: to work or operate something.

market researcher: a person who conducts an organized effort to gather information about target markets or customers.

mason: a person who builds with stone or brick.

mass produce: to manufacture and assemble hundreds or thousands of the same product.

medieval: the period of time in European history between the years of about 350 to about 1450. Also called the Middle Ages.

microchip: a very small piece of silicon that contains the electronic connections for making a computer work.

milestone: an action or event marking a significant change or stage in development.

mock-up: a model of an invention or building.

motif: a decorative design or pattern.

MP3 player: an electronic device that can play digital audio files.

network: a group of computers and related devices such as printers that are connected to each other.

Nichrome: an alloy of the metals nickel and chromium.

ornamental: decorative.

ottoman: a low, upholstered footstool.

patent: a document given to the inventor of something that protects them from someone copying their invention.

pattern book: a book containing samples of patterns and designs for furniture, cloth, and other objects.

peripheral: an accessory designed to work with a main video game console or computer.

pictorial drawing: a view of an object as it would be seen by an observer.

precision: accuracy.

printing press: a machine that presses inked type onto paper.

proportion: the balanced relationships between parts of a whole.

prosthetic: an artificial body part.

prototype: a preliminary model of something.

purify: to make something clean and pure.

rebrand: to change the image or perception of a company or product.

recycled: converted into usable material.

refine: to improve and make more precise by making small changes.

research: the planned investigation and study of something to discover facts and reach conclusions.

revenue: money made by a business from selling products or services.

sanitation: conditions relating to public health and cleanliness, especially clean drinking water and adequate sewage disposal.

scale model: a copy of an object that is usually smaller than the actual size of the object.

scale: the size of something.

sensor: a device that measures and records physical properties.

server: a computer that processes requests and provides data to other computers over a network connection.

sewer: a drain for wastewater.

simulation: a virtual environment that looks, feels, and behaves like the real world.

software: the programs and other operating information used by a computer.

specialist: a person who concentrates on a specific field or activity.

splint: a piece of rigid material used to keep a broken bone from moving after being set.

standardize: to make everything the same.

storyboard: a series of graphic drawings or images that are arranged consecutively to show changes in action or scene.

subassembly: a unit assembled separately but designed to be incorporated with other units into a larger manufactured product.

superimpose: to lay one thing over another.

surplus: more than what is needed.

sustainability: meeting the needs of the present without harming the ability of future generations to meet their needs.

sustainable: designed to minimize environmental impact.

technical drawing: a precise and detailed drawing of an object.

technical: relating to scientific or mechanical methods.

tedious: tiresome, slow, and dull.

terracotta: earthen clay used as a material for buildings, pottery, and sculpture.

texture mapping: the application of patterns or images to the surface of a 3-D model to make it look more realistic.

third-party developer: a company that develops software or games for another company's system.

toxin: a poisonous or harmful substance.

translucent: allowing light to pass through, semi-transparent.

treadle: a lever operated by a foot that causes a machine to move.

trend: what is popular at a certain point in time.

unique: special or unusual.

universal: used or understood by everyone.

user interface: the method by which a user and computer system interact.

vector image: a digital image that is saved in the computer's memory as points, lines, and shapes.

veneer: a thin decorative covering of fine wood.

virtual: a computer version of something real.

virtual reality (VR): not physically existing but made by software to look as if it is real.

visualize: to make something visible.

waste: unwanted material that can harm the environment.

Metric Conversions

Use this chart to find the metric equivalents to the English measurements in this book. If you need to know a half measurement, divide by two. If you need to know twice the measurement, multiply by two. How do you find a quarter measurement? How do you find three times the measurement?

English	Metric
1 inch	2.5 centimeters
1 foot	30.5 centimeters
1 yard	0.9 meter
1 mile	1.6 kilometers
1 pound	0.5 kilogram
1 teaspoon	5 milliliters
1 tablespoon	15 milliliters
1 cup	237 milliliters

BOOKS

Arato, Rona. *Design It! The Ordinary Things We Use Every Day and the Not-So-Ordinary Ways They Came to Be.* Tundra Books, 2010.

Fiell, Charlotte and Peter. *The Story of Design from the Paleolithic to the Present.* The Monacelli Press, 2016.

Fiell, Charlotte and Peter. *Industrial Design: A-Z.* Taschen, 2016.

Lees-Maffei, Grace. *Iconic Designs: 50 Stories about 50 Things.* Bloomsbury, 2014.

Welsbacher, Anne. *Earth-Friendly Design.* Lerner, 2009.

MUSEUMS

Cooper Hewitt, Smithsonian Design Museum: *cooperhewitt.org*
Design Exchange: *dx.org*
The Design Museum: *designmuseum.org*
Madsonian Museum of Industrial Design: *madsonian.org*
Museum of Craft and Design: *sfmcd.org*
Museum of Design Atlanta: *museumofdesign.org*
Museum of Modern Art: *moma.org*
Victoria & Albert Museum: *am.ac.uk*
Vitra Design Museum: *design-museum.de/en/information.html*

WEBSITES

Core 77: *core77.com*
Energy Star: *energystar.gov*
IEEE Computer Society: *computer.org*
Industrial Design History: *industrialdesignhistory.com*
Industrial Designers Society of America: *dsa.org*
Yanko Design: *yankodesign.com*

QR CODE GLOSSARY

page 35: *youtube.com/watch?v=rF_ozSbv-EI*
page 39: *youtube.com/watch?v=BDRjqlPUYNI*
page 41: *coroflot.com/projects*
page 55: *youtube.com/watch?v=IIEb4HcgZ4s*

RESOURCES

QR CODE GLOSSARY (CONTINUED)

page 57: *complex.com/style/2013/02/ the-50-most-iconic-designs-of-everyday-objects/chinese-food-container*

page 62: *slate.com/articles/arts/architecture/2011/10/nice-phone-nice-radio-nice-car.html*

page 62: *ranker.com/list/notable-industrial-designer_s)/reference*

page 62: *industrialdesignhistory.com/timelinebiographies*

page 68: *youtube.com/watch?v=Ze0Az9tdkHg*

page 73: *pong-2.com*

page 77: *youtube.com/watch?v=r9PuSrn_H1c*

page 80: *livescience.com/20718-computer-history.html*

page 80: *computerhistory.org/timeline/computers*

page 81: *dreamstime.com/stock-illustration-set-electronic-circuit-symbols-collection-vector-blueprint-led-resistor-switch-capacitor-transformer-wire-image77183273*

page 81: *startingelectronics.org/beginners/read-circuit-diagram*

page 86: *youtube.com/watch?v=x1rxXm6sG9Y*

page 88: *scan2cad.com/cad/14-top-free-cad-packages*

page 94: *youtube.com/watch?v=FZhwtETwQzs*

page 94: *tinkercad.com*

page 99: *un-documents.net/ocf-02.htm*

page 102: *youtube.com/watch?v=UAxqf5ZAssw*

page 106: *youtube.com/watch?v=--OGJdFF_pE*

ESSENTIAL QUESTIONS

Introduction: What objects have you used today that were influenced by industrial design?

Chapter 1: Why did the world move from craft-based design to mass manufacturing?

Chapter 2: How does having a checklist of design steps make for a better product?

Chapter 3: What characteristics do many designers have in common?

Chapter 4: How does the design of an electronic device affect the success of that device?

Chapter 5: What benefits can beginner designers gain from using CAD? What are the drawbacks?

Chapter 5: What might the future of industrial design look like?